LIES

Everybody's Got Secrets

Shannon L. Guillory

LIES

Copyright © 2012 by (Shannon L. Guillory)

ISBN (978-0-615-81140-6)

Published by Middle Child Publishing Co.

Dedication

All Honor and Glory goes to God the Creator & his wonderful Son Jesus Christ. Everything I am is a result of His amazing Grace. There is no other way, I truly believe that!

Betty Jean Hunt
My own Aunt Betty

"I believe because she believed in me"

Middle Child Publishing
Foreword

"Lies" is the story of a woman, Julia Whitney, whose life unravels after sudden misfortune and a series of bad decisions. She meets a man who causes her life to take a winding road that leads to destruction & turmoil, but ultimately takes both to where they were always destined to be. She is a hardworking straight-laced Real Estate Broker that meets Kevin, who is much less than that. Though not her usual type, he slowly woos her beyond her comfort zone. Kevin appears to be a nice guy but something about him is unsettling at times. He comes along at the most vulnerable time in Julia's life. She begins a relationship with him based on many lies, her own lies and things she's hiding from everyone, and his unimaginable lies which she would never have dreamt possible.

What Julia doesn't know is that Kevin's lies will have a devastating effect on life as she knows it. As the story unfolds, Julia learns more and more about how Lies eventually come screaming at the doors of their owners and how one lie can do more damage than an atomic bomb. On this lustful journey towards love & fortune, Julia will learn how lies can lead to loss, financial ruin, pain, suffering, and sometimes, even death is inevitable.

Preface

Inspired by true events, it was many years ago that this book, Lies, was born. It began as a clever song about the lies of a married man from his mistress's viewpoint. It later grew into a tale of that and much more. Initially, this story would be a drama, but as it evolved, it became a drama, comedy, love story, and mystery.

A true page-turner, Lies took me on a journey I had not imagined and showed me what a writer I can do when the juices of creativity flow freely. I was overcome with joy as I allowed this magnificent story to unfold.

Author

Introduction

I wonder if I can get things back on track, Julia thought. *If only I could have a small break through. Maybe tomorrow will bring some good news. I'll pray and turn in early. I will be well rested, have a nice breakfast and hope God hears me.*

Now I lay me down to sleep, I pray the Lord my soul to keep. If I should die before I awake, I pray the Lord my soul to take. Our father who art in heaven hallowed be thy name thy kingdom come thy will be done. On earth as it is in heaven. Give us this day, our daily bread, forgive us our trespasses and we forgive those who trespass against us. Lead us not to temptation but deliver us from evil. For thy be the Kingdom, the power, and the Glory forever and ever amen.

Lord, please hear my prayers, I thank you sincerely for all that you've done and continue to do in my life. I pray that you give me wisdom and peace over all things. Lord I ask that you bless my mind, soul, and body with renewed strength and purpose. I ask Father that you please bless, keep, and watch over all of my endeavors, and let your will be done. Please Bless and keep my mother, my father, grandmother, aunts & uncles, sisters, brothers, cousins, my friends and my enemies and all of heaven and our earth. In Jesus name, Amen.

Julia prayed her daily prayer and fell quietly off into a much needed deep sleep.

He Stole My Lawn Mower

Julia could hear the doorbell ringing but was trying hard to ignore it. She was running late for work. Julia had missed a few days this week and was hoping to be on time today. She had her music blasting as she moisturized her freshly bathed body with PE360 body lotion, a main part of her morning pre-work ritual. She sang along with the music blaring out of her iPod. She was feeling like her old self for the first time in a while now that she finally received a clear to close on a home loan. Julia couldn't wait to get this deal closed so that she could stabilize her real estate and mortgage company, do payroll, and breathe a little. This deal was huge! She needed it badly.

Julia was on a natural high. She slipped a silky pink blouse over the caramel skin of her ample breast, which glistened as the natural light softly reflected off her mirrors.

As she danced around and prepared to flat iron her dark brown hair...she heard the noise but decided to ignore the constant knocking at her front door. Julia had a rule of never answering her door for uninvited visitors.

Knock knock knock knock knock knock! She heard the person knocking harder and harder and more persistent. She continued to ignore the noise and became more and more annoyed with this intrusion. Knock Knock knock, ding dong ding dong, ding dong, knock knock knock. This person was knocking while simultaneously ringing the doorbell.

"This person is very persistent" Julia said to herself. She was fed up and irritated. She abruptly turned and moved towards the knocking with the intention of letting someone have it good.

"Oh my God! Are you serious? I mean really, is this fool really going to just sit there and lay on the doorbell like that? Oh my God I'm going to rip someone a new ass!" She walk briskly through her bedroom, down the hallway, hit her foot on something, and yelled *"oh shit! Ouch!"* then she hopped past the living room and kitchen until she reached the front door. As she approached the front door, she could see OJ.

"Oh nooooo! I know damn well his ass ain't knocking like that! I know damn well he ain't sitting here on my doorstep uninvited! Ugh!!!" Julia couldn't open the door fast enough. "Ewwww, this numnut! Geez! Let me hurry up and set him straight! That's the last straw! I have told him a thousand times to call first, he has no respect! He can't be that stupid! I don't have time right now for his stuttering ass!"

She partially opened the door and simply sharply spoke to him with expressed annoyance.

"Yeah?" Julia rolled her eyes.
"Hey Baby, what it do?" OJ spoke with a slight stutter and a crooked smile that would melt the hearts of most women.
"Didn't I tell you not to say 'what it do' to me?" Julia mocked him. "Why are you always dropping by? I live alone and it's just not fair! Why OJ? Why!"
"Uh, yeah, uh s s s sorry baby. So what are you doing t today?" OJ stuttered again. Now feeling embarrassed.

"Ok, look. Now listen to me good OJ. This can't continue. So let's just stop now." Julia pushed on his chest as he tried to come in.

"Uh uh uh, what can't continue? Told you I ain't got to say 'wh wh what it do' It's cool, I got chu."

"No! Just listen. We can't see each other like 'that' anymore. I can't have you thinking you can just drop by like this. You never do as I ask you. This will not work. You need to grow up!" Julia yelled as she lost patience with him.

OJ was shocked and confused, his face showed it. He didn't understand why she'd say those things. His eyes watered.

"What do you mean grow up? Can't work? You mean you quitting OJ?" He pointed to himself with no understanding.

"OJ, there's nothing to quit! We are not a couple! We are not dating!"

"Yes we are!" He yelled.

"Come on now OJ, you know I have told you many times I am not interested in a relationship." Julia chuckled.

"Yeah, bbbbut you still hang out with me. I thought--" OJ stopped short as he realized they weren't on the same page.

"Stop that! Seriously, did you really think we'd be a couple? A girl like me being serious about a guy like you? Come on (*she laughed*) we were just having fun *right?*" Julia continued to laugh at OJ's naivety.

"Naw see, I been catching feelings, ain't nobody just having fun girl! Ida married you and made you my wifey yo!"

Laughter then sobering, "Oh my God! You knew what this was! You can't be serious. You're not my type. You had to know this, I told you this!"

"Damn! What about all the stuff I did for you man! (*He threw his body around and pointed to her landscaping*) I ain't taking no losses!"

"What? OJ, you did my yard! I didn't even ask you to do that! And I paid you for doing it! Everyone takes losses in every kind of relationship! Yard work? Really?"

"I ain't taking no losses! I cleaned your garage, your car, this yard, that's all me." He turned a full 180 degrees pointing to all of his work and nearly fell over in his haste and emotional display.

"And you were paid to do most of it OJ!"

"Well I ain't leaving! I ain't letting you quit OJ! What about my flowers? (*He pointed to some flowers and a small tree freshly planted in her garden.*) You didn't pay me for those!"

"Well, everyone takes losses in relationship, consider it yours babe! (*She looked at her watch*) Whew, look at the time. Well, um, sorry, I gotta go. See you around OJ."

Julia slammed the door in his face and he was numb. As he stormed off, one could hear mumbled crying.

"See you around OJ. It's over OJ. Get out OJ. Th th that's alright! Ima show her losses! OJ ain't taking no more losses!"

OJ stormed off to his truck. What most people don't know is that he seems dumb but he's not as dumb as he appears to be. He actually earns a very good living. His landscaping business does very well. His old boss retired and sold it to him. The business already had several large self-sustaining corporate accounts. He does alright for himself. He's about thirty five years old, lives alone, 5 trucks in his landscaping fleet, savings, etc. He's actually not a bad catch. He stands about 5'10" feet tall, good-looking and has a decent body. But then he will open his mouth and ruin it all.

OJ even has a college degree in kinesiology earned at Sam Houston State University where he also played college football for 4 years. Julia figured he stumbled across the degree from playing football on a scholarship. He worked at the landscaping company during his college years.

On his way to an NFL draft (*where he had made first draft pick*) he was injured in an automobile accident. That accident ended his football days but gave him a nice little nest egg from the insurance settlement. He would never play again. He continued to excel in the landscaping business after barely graduating and because he was his boss's personal favorite, the old man basically sold the business to OJ for next to nothing. He was more than he seemed.

Julia called him a lucky fool because he proved that you don't have to be book smart to be smart. He wasn't much different from any other man. When she met him, he lived with a woman he had dated for a few years but didn't want to marry. Shortly after Julia met him, he had moved into his own place and he claimed his ex was the issue with their break up. OJ said his ex's adult son had caused constant conflict in their relationship. He also said she was far too clingy. Julia thought, how ironic, since OJ was a bit clingy to her. He started working on Julia's lawn and did an amazing job. He had coached her on how to do some of the upkeep herself. Julia enjoyed gardening and had visions of a vegetable garden of her own. She just didn't have the time to get it started. They had started as friends. Julia's sisters teased her about their friendship and when she went on the first date, they blew a gasket. They tried forbidding her from dating him. Funny thing is Julia didn't even like him. He was fun and they always had a good laugh. He was very refreshing from her past relationships, so she liked to hang out with him. The more her family disagreed, the more she moved towards him just to prove they couldn't run her life. They always thought someone was using Julia. She never understood why they took her for such a dummy. OJ was no prince charming. Julia liked him because he was the what-you-see-is-what-you-get kind of guy. When they started dating and being intimate, she was more than willing. Julia always reminded him that they were just having fun and that she didn't intend on making this anything serious. He led on that he felt the same way. They went to movies, malls, restaurants, etc. He even took her paintballing! He had taken her to this bar, the Oz Bar, not far from her house with a live band. She loved it! Best wings ever! The bar seemed kind of red-neck-ish, but, it wasn't. The patrons were biker types and cowboys and girls. She was able to throw on jeans and a t-shirt. This was a different look from her usual attire. They would play this silly bar game with these crazy monkeys drinking and falling off the bar stool. Julia would go crazy trying to keep her monkey on the stool. She'd crack up. She was addicted to that game. There was another one with an angry monkey at work who would throw all types of office equipment out of his office window. It was funny and cute. Julia wasn't good with video games but this was a great release for her while her life was falling apart.

She actually was enjoying herself with him, but with as much fun as she was having letting OJ help her escape her reality, their differences were still apparent. It would never have matured into anything else. She had been trying to find the right moment to end this fling. She always postponed it because she didn't want to hurt his feelings. Never did Julia anticipate OJ being so emotional about her ending this fling. After all, she knew he had other things going on. He would say he was always dodging his crazy ex. Julia never felt a person could be crazy about you if you were clear of your motives. Later, Julia learned that he was still creeping over to his ex's house. She didn't make a fuss because she didn't plan on keeping the relationship going and had been looking for the right time to simply break it off. He had been lying about still seeing the ex and that alone was reason enough to just get rid of him. Julia wondered why he couldn't just be honest especially since she was clear of her intentions towards him. As a result, she lost respect for him. Her thoughts were, why do men who are not all that, still play games?

OJ ran to his truck crying real tears. Julia laid her back against her door and exhaled. She wondered if she should laugh or cry. She had already applied her makeup so she decided to keep her emotions intact. Julia had many emotions, beyond OJ, building up inside of her and it didn't take much to break her down to tears. She heard his door slam and went back to her room. Julia felt bad for being so harsh. She wished she could have done it differently or at least invited him in to sit and talk. He might be a liar, but she didn't like that cold side of her. She never thought he would take it hard. All she could think of is the ex he was still seeing anyways, and how verbal she had been of her relationship with him. Her mood went sour as she continued her morning ritual of getting ready for work.

OJ did like her, but, his pride was hurt. He had hoped she'd eventually change her mind but deep inside he knew she never would. He decided to punish her. OJ sobered up, put his truck in reverse and backed up to her garage. He used the side entry because he knew it was always open. He chuckled as he imagined the look on her uppity ass face when she found out what he did. He laughed hard and had to quiet himself so she wouldn't hear him and stop his fun. It was obvious he's not very bright. He rummaged through her garage for things to take to cushion his relationship loss (*as she had put it*). He loaded up all sorts of ridiculous things. Christmas tree ornaments, gift wrap, books, empty boxes.

"Yeah her ass won't be having a damn Christmas with these damn decorations. She damn sho won't be using these boxes!"

Funny thing, OJ was by passing good stuff like lawn mowers, leaf blower, gardening tools, computer stuff and electronics, and other things of value for these ridiculous items.

He was very tickled by his accomplishments. He drove off, but, once he reached her gate to exit the neighborhood, he realized how dumb it was to take those things. She'll never forgive him now, she hates thieves more than a hang nail or bad hair day. Petty or not, she hates thieves and loathes stealing. He once saw her drive back to Golden Coral to return $3 to the cashier who given her too much change. But, he remembered how she said everyone takes losses in relationships. He knew she was done with him and he knew she was clear about it. He got angrier. He parked his truck at the store nearby, walked back to her house fast. He used the garage door opener inside the garage to let the garage door up.

Julia (*almost ready to leave*) heard the noise and lowered the volume on her iPod.

"Hmm, thought I heard something. Dang it! I did! That's my garage door! What th…"

She asked herself the rhetorical question but knew it had to be OJ. She ran to her back door and looked out. She saw OJ but couldn't see his truck or what he was doing. She got her shoes and ran out after him.

"OJ! What do you think you're doing? Wait! Wait? That's my riding lawn mower! Hold on! You can't do that!"

She ran down the driveway after him. OJ kept riding the mower but stopped abruptly at the curb. He yanked up a newly planted tree he planted the weekend before, hopped back on the mower, tucked the tree under one arm, and drove off with the other arm. There Julia stood frozen in shock. OJ put the mower in reverse and she ran towards him.

"Why are you doing this?" She yelled after him.
"Uh Uhhhhhhh, you said everyone takes losses in relationships, con con consider this yours!"

She stood there as he rode off on her mower with her new tree, which she bought herself and he planted. Just like that, he was done with her too. He rode off on the mower onto the main street all the way to his house. Proud of what he had done, still, he would miss Julia Whitney. One lone tear fell from his eyes.

One Night(mare) Stand

After that little stunt by OJ, Julia feared her day would go downhill and so it did.

What an awful day! Julia yelled as she started the engine on her Mercedes. She beat her hands on the steering wheel and rested her hands on her head. She recapped her horrible day. First of all, OJ showed up, tripping and carrying on like they were a serious couple. Geez! She thought. In no lifetime was he in danger of that happening. Then he stole her riding lawnmower. Maybe she was a bit harsh with him? Maybe she should have let him down easy? Nah! She thought, she had done the right thing. She couldn't keep that up.

Then, she got to the title company for the closing only to find out that once again, a lender had closed its door in the middle of closing. They had signed all of the papers and the closing agent came in and informed the parties that the lender won't fund the deal. What! Why not? She said the lender closed its doors and rescinded the wires. They're not funding anything past yesterday. Julia's stomach dropped and it took everything in her not to cry on the spot. She held it together until this very moment.

Julia sat in the parking lot of her office like she had done many times lately, crying her eyes out in hysteria. Every ounce of emotion she had been holding back was now on that steering wheel. As the calm returned she could hear the faint sound of her cell phone ringing. She wiped the tears from her eyes and looked for her cell. She pulled it from her signature Gucci handbag and answered it. It was her attorney and friend, Thomas.

"Hey! Where are you? Come meet me at the spot for a drink or two. Don't say no either! I'm not taking no for an answer, I had the world's most horrible day! It will only get worse if you say no. So you have to say yes." Thomas was already sitting at the bar.

"Ok, I'm on my way, leaving the office now" said Julia.

Julia looked in the rear view mirror, took out her Mac makeup compact and powered her face to look more presentable. She hoped her eyes didn't' look too red or her face too flushed. She dabbed a little blusher on just to make sure.

Thomas had a way of making Julia feel better. So, having a drink with him on this killer day would be a good fit. He was a good friend. Though he was an attorney, he was odd and corky. He acted like every woman in the world wanted him but she knew better. When she met him, he was bad built, probably never lifted a weight his whole life. He was funny looking and would not grab the attention of most women. His shirts were simple and off the rack while his shoes were questionable at best. Probably from JC Penny or Payless, Julia thought. Yet he was cool as shit. He knew all the dances, songs, slang terms, hip-hop, etc. a real camillion. Still beneath it all he was cute.

He was married to an average woman, with an extra-large ego, which was annoying. She didn't care for Julia and Julia didn't care for her for that very reason. When they met, she gave Julia major attitude. Julia was warm and kind to her and in return his wife unleashed an uppity rude sharp tongued attitude on her. That pissed Julia off and she wondered why women were so obviously jealous and for no reason. Thomas's wife was pretty. She wore her hair straight with no style or pizzazz. Her clothes were simple and safe. Compared to Julia's elaborate wardrobe, she was very plain.

Julia wanted to tell her that she had no interest in Thomas and she didn't see him in that way, just to ease her mind. She thought better of it, because deep inside, Julia wanted her to suffer and believe whatever she wanted. She was tired of rude low class females mistreating other women because they feel threatened.

Over the course of Julia and Thomas's friendship, they did great business and became good friends. She had introduced him to her tailor, just as a good friend of hers had done when she first got started. She even suggested he go to Kenneth Cole to pick out some casual clothes and shoes. Julia valued his friendship more than any friend she had. Later, Thomas began working out at the gym in his office building inspired by Julia's dedication to staying fit. She watched him turn into a very good looking attorney. Still, she never looked at him as more than a friend. They did have a kind of flirt-flirt friendship. It was a healthy one though and never led to anything more than a playful flirtation.

She had just arrived at the bar when Thomas called to cancel. He said his wife was in a fender bender and he was on his way to help her. Now fully over this horrible day, Julia rested her head on the steering wheel and exhaled. She lifted her head and decided she would still have one glass of wine, even if she had to do it by herself.

Julia gently pulled her tailor-made black skirt up a bit so that she could hop onto the bar stool. Her hair flowed perfectly in place as if she had just left a salon appointment. She struggled ungracefully to remove her suit jacket which was plain black but custom tailored to fit her every curve. She always accessorized with a watch, bracelet, ring on both middle fingers, and matching earrings with necklace. Her jewels sparkled as the bar lights shined down on her. Her hands were flawlessly manicured and nails always polished in soft earth tones. Julia's white blouse was embellished around the neckline which made her necklace seem overstated yet safe and tasteful. She was notorious for being well dressed. As she sat there, one could see the muscle tone of her arms and legs. She ran 3 to 5 miles each morning and did crunches religiously every day of the week. Some might say she was obsessive about her appearance. She was not conceited though. She just liked to look and feel a certain way. Her elders in her family were all top heavy and this was a major fear of hers. She'd rather work out than get caught with even one extra pound.

At the bar, she sat one leg over the other poised with her wine glass in hand dangling between her fingers. She took the other hand and traced the rim of the glass with one finger and licked the finger often when it seemed to absorb the dampness of the wine. Julia slowly sipped as her glass reduced in wine. The room was filled with people dressed in their work attire. The men could be seen loosening their neck ties as the women adjusted their shirts and combed their hair with their fingers. It was rather loud and to her surprise, actually seemed more packed than usual. Lots of people were talking, laughing, and enjoying. Music filled the room high enough to groove to but low enough to hear and share conversations. Laughter was infectious. It made you want to join in a conversation or two. Julia would have normally found someone to converse with but tonight she wanted to be left alone.

She just sat there and thought about how amusing OJ had looked riding off on her riding lawnmower with that damn tree from her yard. She chuckled to herself. She reminded herself of what a mistake it had been to ever have dated him. Her family never liked him. Her sister knew him and thought Julia was slumming by dating him. They had so much fun together. She really needed the excitement at the time. Julia was already suffering through the crisis of the real estate industry when she met him. He'd been good to her and provided an escape that she needed at the time. He may have even been good for her over those months. He sure as heck was good in bed. Damn, she thought. Now she'd miss the good sex for sure. She had weaned away from him over the last month, which was probably why he popped up this morning. She was feeling very sexy at the thought of those rendezvous she and OJ shared. Julia enjoyed his company and knew full well that she was rebounding from both real estate and from her ex. This would be one of many mistakes she'd make during her real estate crisis.

"Hello Julia." A male voice loomed over her. She turned her head to see who it was.

"Mitchell King! Oh my, how are you?" she smiled a surprised and teasing sexy smile.

"I'm well *(he reached in to hug her, she felt his heat)* and I don't even need to ask how you are *(as he stood back a bit)*, I can tell how you're doing *(he looked her over up and down, curve to curve, breast to breast)*.Umph umph umph. Let me buy you a drink."

"Well, I have one *(she allowed the remaining wine to slide down her throat)*. Besides, I'm done" Julia placed the empty glass on the bar attempting to slide off the stool.

Julia was getting up to leave when Mitch grabbed her arm and coerced her to remain seated.

"Come on" *(he said pleadingly)* have one more with me. It's been a long day baby and I could use the company."

"Well *(the word lingered off her tongue as she could feel the flirting in his voice and his touch. She looked at him with adoring eyes and turned to sit back down)* Well sure, why not, I guess one more won't hurt."

Mitch motioned the bartender to bring her another drink and him as well. They had a few laughs and a few drinks. Julia usually would have only one or two drinks. She found herself enjoying herself for the first time all week long. Mitch King or better called "King" *(his own self-proclaimed nick name)* was about 6 foot 2 inches tall about 205 lean pounds of succulent man. Julia was very picky and hadn't dated much since her big break up with Roger, actually just OJ. In the case of Mitch, she would have been overjoyed to date him. He was good looking, clean cut, smelled good and a nice guy. He knew how to cook, which was something few men knew how to do. Well, except OJ, who was raised by his grandmother and had learned how to cook, clean, sew, etc. Mitchell King had hosted an open house with her before and made some delicious appetizers for the occasion. Julia was very impressed. To date King would be a no no, King was an industry man. She knew better than to date within her industry.

The more they talked and drank, the more she forgot about her horrible day. Mitch was nice. Very funny too! He cracked jokes and had her laughing out loud. Mitch had asked her out on numerous occasions. She always declined. She never wanted to date men in her industry. They thought all realtors were whores so; she made it a point to make sure the word was out that she was out of reach. She had always thought Mitch was a good catch for someone. She knew he was interested in her but she had no plans to date him or any other guy in her industry ever. He was a very successful insurance broker, a work-a-holic to the core. She'd seen him around all the time at networking events and industry functions. Sometimes she'd see him at the grocery store or gas station too. They'd chat a bit but it always ended with him asking her out for a date or inviting her over to his place for dinner which he'd offer to cook for her. He'd call periodically but they'd never actually hooked up. Tonight would be different.

While they sat at the bar, they met several people as well. Everyone was taking shots and eating appetizers. They laughed, told tales, and acted silly at times too, overall, forgetting about all of their problems. Julia was enjoying herself tremendously. As the atmosphere slowly calmed down and the patrons began to scatter, softer music played in the background. The mood changed. It became a romantic setting full of sensual ambiance. Mitch motioned for the bartender and requested 2 cups of coffee. He then placed his hand over Julia's hand and softly asked.

"Julia, why haven't you let me take you out, show you a good time? You have to know I'm interested."

"Yes, I know, but, I'm not interested."

"As far as I know, you're not seeing anyone and neither am I, what is it about me you don't like?"

"I like you just fine Mitch, as a friend and colleague. I'm not interested in anything else. *(She lied)* Is that a crime?"

"I'm not trying to marry you today, I just want to hang out, enjoy each other's company, date, and see what happens. This was nice. Didn't you have a good time?"

"Yes I did. I really did. But let's keep it at that."

Julia felt flushed as if she was blushing. She knew she had desires for him. She actually would date him if he wasn't in her industry. It's like mixing business with pleasure. If it didn't work out, you'd have to see the guy everywhere you went in the line of business. Firmly, she stood on never dating men in the industry. But, like her daddy said, the only cure for one is another. Hind sight, daddy probably shouldn't have taught Julia or the other daughters that one.

Mitch took her hand and placed it discreetly on his very well endowed manhood. Julia just about screamed! She became instantly aroused and sat frozen on the bar stool. She snatched her hand back. He took her hand again; she didn't fight him this time. He rubbed her hand back and forth across the length of his manhood. She just melted! She then groped him with natural reciprocity. Shocked, she allowed her mind to dream. Dreams of a one night stand with Mitch. Oh yeah, she wanted this. She was enticed and curious how he'd feel inside her. She quickly became moist and very ready. He leaned in to kiss her. She withdrew, jumped down from that barstool and headed for the door. He promptly retrieved his wallet from his pocket, dropped cash on the bar fast, and yelled "keep the change" to the bartenders…and chased after her with her purse in hand. Her history was repeating itself, one too many always equaled bad decision making for Julia. Not this time, she thought.

"Julia, wait, you left your purse. *(She stumbled when she realized she wasn't able to leave and must turn back to get her bag from Mitch)* What's the matter with you! *(He yelled at her)* What's the big idea, running off like that, like a scared child? I know you're interested. Truth is, you've been interested and so have I. I can feel the vibe Julia. (*He grabbed her and pulled her into him*) Julia, at least let me drive you home. You're too tipsy to be behind the wheel."

She really knew he was right, she was a little tipsy. Damn, if she had a little more water and coffee and maybe sat a little longer, she would be fine. She couldn't go back in though, she was afraid he'd broken down her barrier. She did want him, and had contemplated dating him. Her terrible day flashed before her eyes and she grew very emotional. She knew she was in financial trouble but did she have to suffer personally as well. More bad decisions sat before her. She needed to feel loved. She was so alone dealing with all of her current drama. The last thing she needed was a DWI too. She tried to rationalize sexing him tonight. At this point, Julia didn't care about being a good girl. She didn't care what the world would think, and right about then, she could care less about a silly rule about not dating industry men. She thought, "To hell with it!"

Julia told herself, he can strap up and hit it and probably give her the best orgasm she'd ever had. So she decided to go there.

"Yes, you can take me home, but, you sure better be worth it. Don't disappoint me." She smiled and so did he.

"Trust me Julia Whitney, *(surprised by her obvious sexual invitation)* I am more than worth it."

His arrogance excited her. He exuded all "man" and she loved that. Julia didn't know it but, Mitch was more excited than she was. He had that same kind of excitement she had twelve hours ago when she was getting dressed for work heading to the closing that wasn't going to happen. He was so chatty on the way to her house. He was eager to please her and knew he'd have her just where he wanted her with this one shot between her lovely legs. He was over joyed and longed to kiss every inch of her. Julia was very intoxicated by him and maybe the wine as well. She had been so much fun all night at the bar. He'd seen a side of her that made him know he could easily fall in love with her. She'd made it clear she was not interested in him over and over and over again, but he knew better and he didn't care. He was hung like a horse, well off, decent looking and had his life together. Even Julia with her reputation for having men fall to her feet, could do a whole lot worse than him. She remained semi-silent all the way to her house, speaking only when she could not avoid it. He had music playing sensually on the radio.

As they drove along, many love songs and ballads flowed softly. Both Julia and Mitch enjoyed the soothing sounds of R & B. Sade's heavenly voice resonated deeply within Julia's heart. She was a hopeless romantic making bad decision after bad decision. Julia's work was a driving force in her life. She was failing badly. Julia knew her latest decisions were detrimental but she seemed to keep needing an escape from her reality. She sure looked as if everything was ok. Her family never understood her. She tried her best to please everyone. Her sharp tongue and quick wit made for an excellent cover-up of her truth. Reality was, if some miracle didn't happen soon, she'd lose everything. Julia had nowhere to turn and no one to turn to. No one knew and maybe no one even cared.

They arrive at her house and she had him pull all the way up her drive way and into her garage. Luckily, she had a remote key fob that allowed her to arm and disarm her alarm without the large car remote. She chuckled as they passed the spot where the tree was missing. Then she burst out laughing. Hell she couldn't stop laughing. She laughed and laughed and laughed. She laughed so hard Mitch started laughing to. Mitch motioned her to her door and helped her with her keys. He just figured she was drunk giggling. She led him to her bedroom, motioning him to take a seat for a sec. Left the room into the master bathroom. She scrambled for a few items and re-entered the room with a towel, toothbrush and other items.

"Let's do this right. These are all new, fresh and unused. I'll use my restroom while you find your way to the guest bathroom. We'll get the "all day" off of us and enjoy each other in say about 10-15 minutes?"

Mitch nodded his head in agreement.

He was wowed as he showered. He thought, "She's a real piece of work. But I sure ain't gonna let my pride get in the way of me getting her" He scrubbed his muscular body head to toe, going over his ripped abs several times. He wondered what kind of shower gel she'd given to him it smelled amazing. Just as amazing as her. The shampoo left him feeling tingly and clean. Man he wanted her more and more by the second. Her house was well decorated and he thought with the naked eye, she hired a decorator, he then remembered when he did her insurance for her mortgage refinance she was in the process of decorating it herself. Man! She had her shit together. He had to have her, to keep her. He made it back to the bedroom to find it clad with candles and fragrance. What was her perfume? He couldn't place it, but knew, no matter where he found himself in this world; if he smelled it…he'd turn and look for her. She was first class all the way. Soft jazz music filled the whole house. Mitch was fully ready from head to toe and everywhere in between. So was Julia.
She was upright in her bed, body glistening in the candlelight. She looked radiant, upright on her knees with the "come get me" look

in her eyes. Oh she wanted it and now she was going to get it. He stood there ready and this is exactly what went down.

"You ready?" Julia asked in an inticing voice, eyes piercing through him.

"Oh yeah!" His voice unsteady and weak.

"Then come get this!"

"You bet. Damn you're sexy! Ooooh weee. I've been waiting for this. Oh I want you so bad. Oh I've been dreaming of this."

"O K, *(she stretched the o and the k in disbelief)* great. Come on then. Get this then." Julia very seductively repeated.

"You bet. Damn you're sexy! Ooooh weee. I've been waiting for this. Oh I want you so bad. Oh I've dreamed of this!"

Mitch embarrassed himself by going on and on like that. He hopped very unattractively onto her bed and landed also on his knees. He grabbed her breast. He was salivating like a wild dog. Ugh! *She thought.* Damn, he was so sexy at the bar. Why is he acting like this? She looked at him in amazement while he embarrassed them both with this pathetic panting behavior. She was losing patience. Then he started nibbling her neck. She relaxed again until...he drew back a bit and cupped her right breast in one hand and slapped it with the other hand.

"Ouch! *(She screamed)* What the heck!" She was pissed.

"Oh I'm sorry, you're so sexy!" Mitched ignored her out cry and continued to kiss her neck.

She let him try again and he repeated the same slapping with the other breast.

She yelled again, "Ouch! Why the hell did you do that?'

"Oh I thought women liked that?"

"My God! No! We don't! Where'd you get that ridiculous idea?"

"Sorry. Damn you're so sexy. Look at you! OoooooWeeeeee! I guess I'm a little excited. I want you so bad! I have dreamed this a thousand times."

Now beginning to tense up, Julia shook her head in disbelief. If he doesn't get to it she decided she would ask him to leave.

"Look, you gonna get this or what? Now, no more slapping or we're done! Now come on." *(Julia had some alcohol induced courage. She was always ballsy but this was new, even for her.)* Encouraging and seductively she cooed, "Give it to me." Julia pulled him closer to her and coerced him on top of her.

She was absolutely breathtaking. Mitch never stood a chance. Julia, in all of her arrogance, made men weak. They'd start off strong but something about her arrogance matched theirs. Her demeanor took them off guard. She was soft, gentle, sexy, and sensual. Then there was also abrasiveness about her. She came across at times as cold and disinterested, like she could care less if you lived or died. That side of her was mostly her business side or the side that was her self-defense mechanism. There was an air of confidence that captivated them. Mitch lost his edge in her presence. Why did he go weak on her? He just kept complimenting her, over complimenting her, salivating at the mouth as he took her beauty in.

Her soft caramel breast covered in the silkiness of her bra and panty which matched her beauty. She smelled nice. Mitch wanted to just stand there and soak it in, soak her in, breathe her in. He wanted to inhale her and lost all sense of where he was or what they needed to be doing at present. Never in his life had he been so smitten. He hadn't started his day with this in mind. Julia showed no sign of weakness, ever. Yet she was weak at heart and just longed for a good solid relationship with a man of her stature. Maybe she was too picky. Still, she was willing to wait for the not-so-perfect guy who would be perfect for her.

"Oh baby my pleasure!" Mitch's chuckling was cute. "Yeah lets."

He climbed on top of her and began kissing her neck. It felt good to her. He was touching her all over. She was ready. Even in spite of the breast slapping, she didn't want to turn down what she felt would be amazing. She was always attracted to him and tonight that attraction would breathe life into their relationship. She was open to the outcome, again moving too fast. She'd never had a one night stand and rationed with herself that this doesn't constitute as a one night stand because she knows him. Tonight whether it's the wine or not, she would have her first and probably last one night stand. Maybe they'd see each other even after. Julia didn't care. She played it safe all through college when her friends were all doing what college students do. She couldn't bring herself to have sex outside of a relationship then, and felt this would balance the scale a bit.

She could feel the warmth his manhood getting closer to her entry point down there. She pushed him up.

"Wait! Where's the ummm, you know?"

"What?" He asked as if he didn't understand he needed a condom to be with her.

"What? The condom you moron! You have one right?" Julia Was beginning to get angry by the second.

"No baby, I don't have one. Besides, I trust you. I know you don't have anything."

He leaned in to kiss her some more. Right there, he lost her. She would never ever consider having sex with anyone without a condom. What the hell was he thinking? Trust her? She grew down right angry with those words coming from his lips! The lips she let kiss her. She couldn't have been more insulted.

"I'm glad to know you trust me but I don't trust you! Get off me! Now! Get off me! *(She was beating him off of her and hopped up shouting)* Get off of me and get out! How could you come all the way to my house for sex, slap the shit out of my tits, both of them! Talk wayyyyy too much! Then try to get it without a condom! Really?" By this point she had her bathrobe on.

"Calm down *(reaching out to her with both hands, he pleaded with her pulling away)* it's cool, I didn't think about it. Say, wait, don't you have any condoms?"

"No! Just leave! Now, please leave" Julia's arms were folded and she was serious as hell. She wanted him gone. He ruined the night.

"Well, can't I just run to the corner store real quick?"

"No, you can't, you had your shot! I'm not waiting while you go to the damn store*! (She grabbed his belongings and shoved them at him)* How many stores do you figure we passed between the Galleria and here? Damn! Please go!"

Julia motioned him towards her door and through the hall way. He was getting dressed as fast as he could. She was pretty alert now and very disgusted. He was kind enough to just obey her.

"I guess there's no chance of us hooking up again anytime soon is there?" Mitch embarrassed himself even more.

"Hell no! Bye Mitch!"

Julia was very pissed off. She didn't have words. Mitch called her several times. He even rang her door bell a few times. She figured he must have gone to the store and bought condoms. She ignored him. How could she be so stupid? She had never done anything like this. She figured she deserved the results. She could just kick herself. Sure she was a grown ass woman, but, certainly she didn't have to prove it like this. She replayed the evening. She knew she had her own condoms but it was the principal. Did Mitch honestly think he'd get her in bed without a condom? To that she showered, again, and went to sleep as fast as she could happy to close her eyes on the worse day ever!

Best Friend, Ex Friend

The next day Julia slept in. She dreaded going to work. She decided to go when everyone else had left already. She didn't want to face the sad faces and curiosities of her employees.

She finally got up the courage to face the music and she headed to her office. She had to drive her convertible because she'd let Mitch drive her home. She knew she could just have Ronnie take her to get her car and follow her home to drop off the convertible. She felt stupid.

She arrived back to her office just after business hours. Julia sat patiently waiting for Erica to call her back. Erica was her best friend and business partner. They weren't really business partners but worked in Julia's office together. She was a loan officer, very good at her job. Julia had been going over the recent client intake sheets and noticed that everyone was denied for a loan. She also noticed that there were no recent approvals for the last month. She was very worried about the decrease in business. There she sat, tapping her fingernails on her desk. Something just didn't feel right. It had a funny feeling in the air at her office. Julia had put everything into advertising. She was very concerned that the monies she was putting out were in no way paying off or bringing about a return. Why was she getting so many people with bad credit? It just didn't add up. Ronnie was always so optimistic. Then again optimism was Ronnie's middle name. She'd make a black eye into a birthmark, pneumonia into a common cold; she'd even minimize a hurricane into a little rain.

Could Ronnie be that off? She was interviewing the clients over the phone. Even Julia reviewed the files before the clients came in for the appointments. Just didn't add up. So, again she called Erica and got no answer. Crazy, but, usually Erica answered all of Julia's calls. She was beginning to get worried. She called her house and Erica's husband, Greg, said she wasn't there. Even he sounded a little off. Greg was always out of order more so since Julia's breakup with his best friend. Ever since the break Greg seemed to act differently towards Julia. They were all close and they each suffered when the breakup happened. It had been a long time ago though. Could he still be holding it against her? "Who cares" she thought. He never treated Erica right anyway. He was rude, arrogant, and a real a-hole most of the time. But, still Julia kind of liked him; she appreciated him being exactly what he portrayed to be. Still, she couldn't help feeling something was wrong, he sounded guilty or like he was lying.

Julia decided she'd better have a look at the credit reports and see if there might be an alternate program the clients could fit into. Subprime loans were a challenge, but, some banks were still lending, maybe even FHA could be a good fit. She knew she'd have to outsource it and Erica wouldn't make her money. Well, if no loan was done, no one would make any money. She had to review those credit reports. She got up from her desk and went to the next office which belonged to Erica. She turned the knob and realized it was locked. She went to get her key ring, came back and retrieved the key to Erica's office. She inserted the key and nothing happened. The key didn't work. Julia tried it again. Nothing. The key didn't work. She checked the key again, nothing. She closely looked at the key and yes, it was the correct key. Puzzled, she went back to her office and sat down. She tapped the desk intently with her finger nails as she grew hot with anxiety.

She sipped her water as her mind raced a million miles. Her blood pressure rose and she almost began hyperventilating when…

The phone rang. Julia answered.

"Hey Erica, what's up? You ok? I've been calling you for Hours" Julia was still oblivious to the obvious.

"Yeah I'm fine, just out and about didn't hear the phone. What's up?"

"Oh, well I was calling because I didn't understand why no one was being approved for loans these past couple of weeks. But now I just tried to get into your office to see the credit reports and I can't get in. Did you change the locks?"

"Oh, yeah I did." Erica's voice was rushed and shallow.

"Well why? And where's my copy of the new key?" Julia was tired of Erica's casual responses.

"Uhh I lost my keys last week and I was afraid someone would use it so I changed the locks."

"What? I never heard you mention it Erica! Why didn't you tell me you lost your key? Where's my copy. I need those reports tonight. Plus what about the main office door key. We should have changed that one too then. Right?"

"Oh, well Julia, I'm in the neighborhood and I can't come back tonight my husbands on my ass because he's been calling me too. Can we please settle this in the morning? I really need to get the kids ready for bed. Is that ok?" Ignoring the questions about the changed locks.

"Well I guess so, but I am still disturbed about the clients all being denied over the last few weeks. What's going on?" Temporarily, Julia forgot about the changed lock issue.

"Damn Julia, we've just been getting some bad ones."

"What about the Johnsons, they said they had good credit. What happened to them?"

"No, I think their scores were low too."

"Really, what were their credit scores then Erica?"

"Uh I don't remember by heart, but, I think low 500's. I'll show you tomorrow. I gotta go. Oh and be careful. You're getting out of there now aren't you? It's late for you to be there by yourself Julia."

"Yeah, I guess I can't do anything anyways, ok, see you tomorrow. I'll be careful."

They both hung up. Julia sat for a moment then grabbed her purse and keys. She figured nothing could be done tonight so she'd better head home. She got to her front desk and paused. Something was nagging at her. She froze at the front desk. Julia turned to look at the visitor sign-in sheet and picked up the clip board to have a look. She saw that quite a few clients had been signing in and that there were telephone numbers on there as well. She went back to her office, sat down, and picked up the phone to call the clients. Something smelled rotten and she was about to get to the bottom of it.

The phone rang several times, too many times. Julia was just about to hang up when a child answered.

"Hello who is this?"

"Hi sweetie, is your mommy or daddy there?"

"Ok, daddy is here mommy is gone."

"Ok." Julia smiled. "Please give your daddy the phone. "

"Ok, thank you bye."

"Hello."

"Hi is Mr. Rodriguez in please?"

"This is he, who's calling."

"Hi I'm Julia Whitney, I apologize for it being a little past business hours. I am the Broker for Whitney Realty. I was just following up with you regarding your visit to our office. I wasn't in today and needed to make sure you were well taken care of."

"Oh yes, hi there. Thought you were a telemarketer. Yes, we were taken care of just fine. Your staff was wonderful and kind. My wife hasn't made it back yet, long day.

"Oh that's great. I'm sorry is your wife out with one of our office personnel."

Julia's heart began to race. It beat so loud she just knew the man could hear it. Her hands were wet with perspiration and she wasn't a sweater. She was so nervous she could just burst.

"Yes, the realtor. She's out with the realtor Erica. They found 2 nice ones but my wife is quite the hand full and wanted to see one more. She'll decide which one she wants, I will go see it and sign the papers tomorrow. She's very excited."

"Oh I see. Well thank you so much for your time Mr. Rodriguez, we appreciate you and congratulations on your approval for your new home."

"Oh great and you're welcome. You guys are the best!"

So there was the truth. Erica did lie to her. How could she? Julia had encouraged Erica to get her mortgage license and she even set Erica up in her office. She brought her in with her when she needed a new career and Julia needed a reliable source for her clients. She thought they were best friends. Julia knew Erica was cut throat in business but she never figured Erica's wrath would turn to her. Now all Julia could think of is how she could have been so dumb to fall for Erica's lies. How many clients had she stolen? But, who did Erica put down as their realtor? Who showed the house, she's not a realtor! Julia sponsored a number of realtors, but, never allowed them into her private world or into her office. She had a section set up for agents to use. They could even use the same desk each day but they never had the level of access that she'd given Erica. Erica's office was right next to Julia's; she had a key to Julia's office, access to all of Julia's company financials, client files, etc. Everything! She had to get into Erica's office and it had to be tonight before the open of business tomorrow.

She grabbed her rolodex and called her locksmith. They said they'd be there in 3 hours or less and it would be just about double the normal cost. That meant she would be at the office until extra late, she was tired but very wired up. She'd have agreed to stay all night if it meant she could get into the office before the morning. She sat patiently and went from desk to desk of every office staff turning on their computers to see what they'd been up to. She checked to see if there were any other trails of deception. She even checked Ronnie's computer. To her surprise, Julia found out that one of her processors, Mark, had pictures of her on his computer. She was appalled. He had photos of her legs, feet, hands, lips, hundreds of pictures of her. That scoundrel! She thought. She gave him a second chance! He was an ex-con and she figured he needed someone to believe in him. How'd he get these pictures, she didn't know. Best she could guess was that he's always on that damn cell phone. He must have been taking them while waiting for her to get off the phone, while she was conducting meetings, etc. They were very alarming and now she viewed him as a stalker. Yuck! Now she was really offended and pissed off. She was about to scream when she heard knocking on the door.

Just a second, she yelled out. She was trying to delete the photos, but couldn't do it fast enough. She left it for later and ran to open the door. She peeked out of the peep hole and asked,

"Who is it?"
"It's me, Wayne, the locksmith."
"Ok." She unlocked the door and let him in.

Wayne the locksmith was in his mid-fifties, he was maybe 5'8 or 5'9 in stature. His hair was salt and pepper while his face was unaged but worn. He had a no-nonsense stance and seemed very professional. He got right down to business.

"Hello ma'am, I assume you're Julia Whitney?"
"Yes I am. How are you?"
"I'm good. How are you? (*Not waiting for an answer and looking at his paperwork*) Let's see here. Looks like you need a new lock?"
"Well sort of (S*he walked towards Erica's office*). You see I need to get into this door. It's locked and I don't have the key. I never authorized the person to change the locks and I need access tonight."
"Oh I see. Ok, let me have a look here."

Wayne looked analytically at the lock and pulled out some tools. He obviously took his job very seriously and was moving about like a surgeon at work.

"I'll have you in here in no time. Be a few minutes."

Julia nodded and gave Wayne the Locksmith some space. She resumed the task of deleting the offensive pictures of her that had been kept on Marks computer. After about 20 minutes Julia returned to the room. She watched as Wayne the locksmith aggressively tried over and over to pry his way into the door lock. He was having some trouble and Julia grew worried. He was sweating profusely which repulsed Julia and made her frown at his drippings.

"Wayne, I hate to disturb you, but, I sense you're having some trouble with that lock."
"Yes ma'am. How bad do you want in?"

As he lifted himself from the floor onto his feet, Wayne wiped the sweat from his face with a towel from his pocket. He smiled at her patiently as he awaited her reply.

"What do you mean! Of course I want to get in bad, that's why I'm here in the middle of the night. I'd do anything to get in there." Her voice was impatient and troubled.
"I thought so. In that case, I will just break the lock and put on a new one."
"Oh no! I can't have it look like I broke in! I need to get in without showing any signs of having been in there. What's the problem? I thought you said it would take just a few moments."

"Well I don't know what to tell you ma'am. There's a small problem. I cannot get this lock opened or get in without breaking the knob or lock. This is a very delicate lock and I've never seen it before. I tried everything except one thing. I can come back tomorrow with some heavier artillery if you like."
"Damn! Ok, I need in there tonight! Wayne please there has to be something you can do to help me tonight." Tears rolled from her face; she went on as if she didn't notice them. "Please help

me. All the cards are against me and my gut tells me that my colleague is stealing business from me. It has to be tonight. But, if there's a 1% chance I am wrong, I just can't break the lock. Please…"

"Ms. Julia, (*he interrupted her*) let me look around a bit."

He looked around the room. He looked really long and hard. Then he spoke.

"Ok, so you really want in there? You said you'd it has to be tonight. Will you really do anything to get in there?"

"What tha!" She wiped her eyes as shocked overtook her face. She drew back as if he'd made a sexual advance towards her.

"Oh no! Wait! You think I? You assumed? No ma'am. I only meant I have another idea. (*He pointed to the ceiling*) Ms. Julia. Is that your office right here? He pointed to her office door as he walked in."

"Yes, yes it is." She followed him curiously.

"Hmmmm." He looked up at the ceiling then tapped the credenza against the wall and hopped onto the credenza. "Ma'am. I have a solution but you're not going to like it. Then again you seem pretty desperate so maybe you'll go for it."

"I'm listening, go on." Relieved that he wasn't making an advance, Julia folded her arms and hung onto every word he said.

"Look, Going over this wall through these ceiling tiles is the only way in there tonight. No one will know but you and me. Only one catch though, what's on the other side of this wall?"

"A credenza. Why? What's the catch Wayne?"

"Great, a credenza is just what we need. The problem is, I won't fit, but you will."

"You expect me to go over through the ceiling and onto the other side. Me? How will I do that Wayne! Seriously? That's the only way?"

"I don't like it either. But I checked and I won't fit but you're small enough. I could boost you up there and make sure you get down safely. Then you just unlock it from the inside, simple."

She walked over to the credenza, looked up at the ceiling tiles, paused, and then looked to the floor then back up at Wayne.

"So, you'll help me Wayne? You see I have a skirt on right?"

"Ma'am I am a happily married man with children your age. Daughters your age at that, and could lose my job for even suggesting such a thing let alone helping you do it. I feel bad for you, still do. It's obvious you're in a bad way and I wouldn't make it worse by taking advantage of you or not helping you. I promise I will do everything in my power to be only a ladder to you. In Christ's name, let me help you so you can have some peace."

"Thank you Wayne, I appreciate your kind words. Let's do this. She held out her hand and he shook it."

Wayne's face was sincere. He wore a cross around his neck. She figured he was a Christian man, looked honest enough and what was the most he would see, panties and some ass? She didn't have much of a choice. She kicked off her shoes. Wayne helped her up onto the credenza. He jumped up there as well. He boosted her up to the ceiling with ease and she grabbed onto the ceiling rails as he held her tightly. He placed his hands on her bottom apologizing the entire time. Julia burst into laughter every time he apologized. He was sweet to place himself in that position with her. Once she was in the ceiling, Wayne coached her through lifting the ceiling tile in Erica's office. Julia made a loud thump when she landed on the credenza. She wasn't hurt but had white ceiling tile remnants and powder on her red skirt and everywhere else. Again she laughed her infectious laugh.

"Julia, are you alright? That didn't sound too good."
"I am fine Wayne. Here I come now, I'm opening the door." She chuckled softly, trying to compose herself.
"Ok, great!" He was relieved she was ok. He would have just died if she'd have hurt herself. He couldn't imagine what he was thinking telling her to try this stunt.

"Whewww" Julia let out a sigh of relief as she opened the door. "Now I have seen it all now and done it all too" She laughed at herself.

Wayne the locksmith smiled and patted her on the shoulder. He looked proud of her.

"Wow! You're one tough lady Ms. Julia. Guess I'll be going if you don't need anything else."
"No, wait."

She reached for her purse, handed him the fee plus a $100 tip. He pushed it back towards her.

"No ma'am. Consider it a gift. I sense you have a long road ahead of you (*he looked around at her office proudly*). Looks like you have a very successful business and lots of wealth. I bet you're a very hard worker."
"Thank you, I like to think I am." She looked puzzled, wondering where he was going with his words.

"You know, the funny thing about judging things according to the way they look is, you miss an opportunity to be a blessing to someone. Things are not usually as they seem, are they Ms. Julia? You're a nice lady. I know you could use a break. I don't have much, but, my small company can afford to be a Blessing to you. Best wishes and God Bless you!"

Wayne walked out swiftly before Julia could process his words or respond. Julia looked at the closing door. She went to it and locked it. She rested her back against the door and accepted the blessing. She thanked God because in all honesty, she didn't have the fee or the tip to spare, but would do what was necessary to put this feeling of doubt to sleep. She was grateful for this huge Blessing. She thought, little did Wayne the locksmith know, he was the biggest Blessing she'd had in a long time.

Julia returned to Erica's office. It was very junkie and messy as hell, she thought. She could never get control over this part of her office. It was awful! Erica was an avid coffee drinker and spilled coffee on client files and paperwork, and always left coffee mug rings on the desk. Julia finally had Erica get a glass desk because she had ruined the wooden desk. She sat in Erica's chair wondering where to start. She looked through a few papers but nothing stood out. After weeding through several stacks of papers, Julia struck gold. She had a grand idea. She would compare the sign in sheet with the mortgage inquiry log then look in Erica's computer for the credit reports.

"Oh my God! I can't believe it (*she yelled out loud).*
She has been lying about the credit scores!"

More than half the clients from the past two weeks had qualifying credit scores for a home loan. The employment experience and rental history appeared to add up as well. Why had Erica lied when Julia had specifically asked what the scores were? She remembered how Erica dodged the lock change questions. She concluded that Erica didn't lose her keys at all and had changed the locks to cover her tracks. She guessed Erica assumed that Julia was stupid or at least too stupid to catch on to her deception and lies. Julia didn't know what to do next. She was very puzzled. She decided to call a few more of the clients. Test the waters and see what information they were told. She started with the Johnsons.

"Hi there, Mr. or Mrs. Johnson in?" *Another kid? Why are these kids answering phones! Geez!*

"Hello. Who is this please?" Probably a preteen on the other line, Julia disturbing her call.

Before Julia could answer, she smiled when she heard a man's voice say, give me that phone! I told you about answering this phone!

"Hello, Mr. Johnson? Is that you Mr. Johnson?"

"Yes, this is Mr. Johnson, how may I help you?"

"Hi, my name is Julia Whitney of Whitney Realty & Mortgage. I wanted to speak to you or your wife if possible about your home loan."

"Oh yes, hello. Is everything ok Ms. Whitney?"

"Yes, everything is fine. I do apologize for the hour, but, we usually feel we can reach clients after dinner so we try to call then. I was wondering how your appointment went today we always follow up after office visits to make sure staff handled clients to the best of their ability."

Nothing prepared Julia for what Mr. Johnson would say next. This was a dark road that would change Julia's life forever and the direction of her company.

"Everything went fine. We felt the interest rate could have been lower, all things considered, but we were able to feel comfortable in the end. The house we found today was everything we'd hoped for and hopefully it's a done deal. The contract signing went fine, the new home sales rep you guys took us to was amazing and assured us we could bring the earnest money cashier's check back by on tomorrow. We decided not to go back today as we had the kids with us. You know how it is with small children. They just won't sit still sometimes."

Julia fell silent. What did he mean contract signing? What did he mean new home sales rep? What's going on? Did Erica really take them out without telling her? Well, maybe she told the builder Julia was their agent. Ok, maybe that's it, Julia thought.

"Hello, hello, Ms. Whitney? Hello?"

"I'm sorry, our connection was bad for some reason (*Julia had zoned out while thinking about what to say next*) Mr. Johnson, I am a bit surprised you went out so soon but I am pleased you're happy. I will let the builder know tomorrow that I'm your realtor."

"No ma'am, (*cutting her off*) we went out with a realtor today, was there some kind of miscommunication?"

"Oh, yes there must have been. I am the only realtor for walk in clients unless I reassign you and I didn't. Who did you go out with today?"

"Let me get her card, one moment."

Julia could hear commotion and rumbling. She grew impatient but concealed it when he returned. Her heart was beating fast again.

"Whew, sorry about that taking so long. Let's see here, her name is Erica Boudreaux real estate agent at All Star American Realty. Do you know her?"

Julia sat perfectly still, she had a thousand things going through her head right now. Why would Erica steal from her at a time like this!

"Yes, I do. I apologize; I didn't know she was your realtor. It's fine sir. Again, I just wanted to make sure all was perfect and it seems to be. Thank you for your time. Have a good night."

"Ok, great. I was worried for a minute there. Same to you and thank you guys for everything. We're very excited. Good night."

So there it was. The writing was on the wall. Julia finally put two and two together. Erica was one of the reasons her company was failing. Erica was double dipping. Julia went on the real estate commission's website and found that Erica had held a real estate license for over a month and said nothing. Probably, because she was stealing business and didn't want Julia to be watching for it. Julia had been so caught up in the downside of real estate she had missed things going on right in her own office. Who could she trust if not her best friend? Well ex-best friend.

Julia took the all of the credit reports and files she could gather and went calmly home. No tears just total silence all the way home.

The next morning, she was the first to arrive at the office. She sat at her desk poised for what was about to go down. She was waiting for Erica Boudreaux. She briefed Ronnie, her lovely assistant, on Erica's soon to be departure but minimized the details as to why.

Erica arrived and was startled when Julia called out her name. Julia couldn't see it but, Ronnie was standing right there when Erica passed by. Erica had a look of shock when she looked towards her own office door and saw it was already opened. Ronnie was curious as to why Erica looked like a deer in headlights. Julia had not shared the full story with Ronnie and Ronnie knew not to pry about details.

"What's up chic? How's it going? Why are you here so early? Not like you ma" Her words struggled to leave her mouth. She seemed curious as to Julia's state of mind. Julia was unmoved and emotionless.

"Come in Erica, close the door."

"Oh, I'm kind of in a rush, can it wait?"

Julia got up walked directly towards Erica, passed her up and closed the door behind them. She pointed to a chair for Erica to sit in.

"No actually it's urgent."

"Ok Julia." Shocked by Julia taking such authority and was about to get defensive "Oh, should I be worried? What's wrong with you? Someone die? You mad about something?" Julia cut her off as she continued to speak.

"Now look, I won't beat around the bush. You've been lying about clients getting approved for loans; you've been taking them out to find houses using my realtor key and codes. Why?"

"Where'd you get that wild information from?"

Julia slammed the files and paperwork down on the desk.

"Right here, in black and white. Why Erica why?"

"Come on Julia (she w*iped her hand over the length of her face from forehead to chin)*. Look, I never meant to hurt you or steal from you. They're not your clients. They are mines. I put some ads in the papers too and they called off my ads, not yours."

"Not true. Do you have a reason why you didn't tell me you have a realtor's license?"

"What you've been spying on me now?"

"Erica, Really? You're going to sit there and play games?"

"Please! Julia are you trying to say you would have been ok with me getting my realtors license? You would have let me still work here? Sponsored me?"

"It's not a matter of me letting you do anything. You obviously don't need my permission. Yes of course I would have supported you! Yes, I would have sponsored you but, no you wouldn't have needed to "work here". My agents work in the field and use the agent's rooms when needed. My agents don't have access to all my stuff. My agents don't run my clients credit reports. You broke my trust. Either way you slice it, you stole from me and I want you out today, now!"

"What? Out? What do you mean out? You don't mean that? Come on Julia, think this through please. I…"

"Erica, I want you out now, I will send your things. I can't stand a thief and I can't stand to look at you for another minute. OUT!" Julia trembled as those words left her mouth.

"Ok, ok! But, what about us, you're my best friend. I know you're not going to throw us away over money Julia?" Loudly, in disbelief.

"No I'm not, you already did. Good bye Erica." Julia stood her ground and braced herself against her desk for strength.

Erica snatched her purse off the chair and headed to her office. She was grabbing a few personal things when Julia came in her office. Julia told her to not remove any files and that she could trust her to send everything that was not Whitney Realty property.

Erica left and it took Ronnie to point out that she was emotionless. Not a tear, not a sad face, not a reaction to any of it. Ronnie described Erica's demeanor as unaffected. She said Erica looked almost smug. Sad, in one twenty four hour period, Julia would lose more than money; she'd lose her right hand man and best friend. Funny thing was, she didn't shed a tear either.

Decisions Decisions Decisions

If this market gets any worse, I'm going to lose everything. *Julia thought as she went over her bank statements.* She would need to liquidate her IRA account, CD's, and personal holdings. She realized she was in trouble. She hadn't profited a dime in 6-9 months. It was a warm March day in Houston. She could feel springs beginning. Pretty bad how the humidity played kick ball with her hair. Luckily, she was in for the day, working from home.

Julia wasn't actually working, but hiding from work, payroll, bills, etc. She had always had money come so easy for her company. She even kept a nice amount in reserve but she was now knee deep in spending her life savings. She needed to recreate the wheel and figure something out. She was spending nearly 20k a month trying to hold on to her good credit, assets, and that company of hers. Julia had grown fast in her 15 years in the industry. She had 4 offices citywide, up until recently. Now as she sat buried in her finances and bills, Julia wondered if she'd make it through this year. Lenders were closing their doors left and right. She had only closed a couple of deals this year. Over the last year she'd broken up with her longtime boyfriend, her best friend (over money), and was in jeopardy of losing her company if things didn't change soon.

Thomas was knocking at her door. He graduated top of his class from Texas Southern University School of Law. He took a liking to Julia years ago when they met at a real estate mixer. As she walked to the door she wondered who it could be. As she got closer to the door, she could see his silhouette through the glass.

Oh no! Oh my God, who is it now! Approaching the door, she saw it was Thomas. She opened the door.

"What are you doing here?"

"Well, I had to come check on my favorite client and good friend didn't I?" He grabbed her and gave her a hug, she did not reciprocate and her arms dangled in the embrace. "Why are you home Julia?"

"Just working from home, hibernating a bit so I can think." Moving them towards her living room sofa.

"Look Julia, I know you're having some tough times and I hate to tell you this. But it's going to get worse before it gets better. You've got to start considering downsizing like we spoke about. It's just unrealistic to try to hold on and end up losing everything. I came by to…"

"Ok Thomas. I appreciate you coming all the way out here and I know where your heart is (*as she urged him back towards the front door*). But I'm ok. I've got deals working. I'll be just fine."

"Wait, at least let my buy your fine ass a drink or some dinner later tonight to make up for sticking you out the other night."

"No, go home to your pregnant wife." She laughed as she pushed him through the door and towards the porch.

"Come on! Can't I redeem myself? I'll leave but meet me later?"

"Fine!" She smiled and shook her head. "Grand Lux?"

"Alright beautiful see you there around 7 tonight." Thomas chuckled as he walked away and waved from behind.

He got into his car and drove away as she watched. Julia closed her door and locked it. She leaned against the door and thought to herself. *What does he think? I didn't answer his calls so he can just pop by! Was that a way of coming on to me. She felt silly thinking like that. He came out because she was in rare form, missing work all the time and not answering calls. She was a mess.*

She knew her thoughts were ridiculous, he was a good friend and that was it. She was visiting a very dark place within herself to have such thoughts. Julia thought back to one day, few years back, when she and Erica went to a networking event. They chatted with Thomas and another friend in the business and enjoyed a few drinks. Thomas was such a ham he kept them all laughing all night. Afterwards, he offered to walk her to her car. She could handle one to two drinks but people were buying rounds and Julia had maybe 2 – 3 martinis. She drank coffee to balance her drinking and felt fine. Erica had left earlier than her so, Thomas had offered to see her to her car.

They were in the parking garage when he went to open her door. He started flirting and then as he opened the door for her he leaned in and kissed her on the lips. She didn't reciprocate but backed away laughing. She urged him to back off and he did. She sat down in the car and when she went to move her left leg into the car he stooped down and tried to kiss her again. Julia scolded him and asked him what the hell he thought he was doing. He apologized and moved back then she slammed her car door and drove off. They didn't speak for a month. Finally, they ran into each other at a title company. It was as if nothing ever happened and they picked their friendship up where it had left off. They never spoke of the incident. Not even up to now.

A few hours had passed when Julia showered and threw on a dress then headed to her office. The walls were closing in on her.

At the office, Julia's assistant Ronnie was deep in thought. She was an exceptionally pretty girl beyond her barely there make up application. She was actually very striking. Ronnie's long brown hair and deep brown eyes set the tone for the natural beauty she was. She didn't really need makeup for a person to notice her beauty, but, when she wore it, she was even prettier. Julia had known ten years ago when she hired her that she'd be a good fit for a personal assistant. Ronnie knew all about the company, Julia's family, her ex, and the boyfriends/dates she's had over that time period.

The best thing about Ronnie was that she never initiated conversation about anything except work. She was a prize. Her discretion was both needed and appreciated. Ronnie had helped Julia build an amazing empire. Julia never took the time to notice that Ronnie had problems of her own. She was married to a man of no certain status. He was a hard worker but for some reason never could catch a break. As a result of his bad luck, Ronnie's husband treated her like crap. Ronnie longed for the passion she saw in other relationships. Even the glimpse of happiness she overheard in Julia's life made her hopeful. She knew Julia had dating troubles but at least she seemed alive. She sat at her desk, looking in the mirror that Julia kept at every desk in the office so that the office staff was always reminded to care about their personal appearance and facial expression when they were on the phone with clients. Ronnie stared at her long brown hair and considered getting highlights. She studied her big brown eyes and thought of green contact lenses. She brushed her hands over her cheeks and wondered if she needed more make up. Ronnie never felt pretty. She didn't even act like it. She could hear Julia's voice encouraging her to trade her glasses for contacts. She wondered what her husband Herberto was doing now that he was laid off again. She was curious if he'd notice if she did any of the self-alterations she had thought of. Was he having an affair? Well you'd have to leave the house for an affair wouldn't you?

"Hello! Ronnie? Are you asleep? *(Laughter)* What's going on around here?"

"Oh I'm so sorry I was day dreaming." She looked up at Julia like a deer in headlights. "Oh no forgive me." As she put away the mirror, makeup, and hair brush. "I'm sorry are you upset?"

"No, I'm not upset. Of course not! Come on." Julia gave her a Sarcastic look. "I need to know how the title searches are coming on these clients. Why is it taking so long anyway?" She handed some files and paperwork to Ronnie.

"I keep calling, only two are in, Alexander and Washington are in. Hall and Cannon are not in yet. I've already got the packages in to Morgan Lending on Alexander and Washington but haven't heard back yet." Ronnie called off the last names of their clients.

Julia stood there looking worried, thinking of the rumors of Morgan Financial closing their doors soon. Her eyes filled with tears.

"Ms. Julia, you ok?"
"Yes, I will be in my office."

Julia sat in her office for what felt like hours. She reviewed the payroll, calculated the utility bills for the office and transferred more money from her savings to the operating account for Whitney Realty. She was afraid to spend a single dime on herself. Julia lived a very lavish life. She always valet parked if it was offered, fancied every high end shoe store in town, loved a good custom suit, loved to visit the salon weekly, and networking was a staple in her life.

"Julia?" *Ronnie stood in Julia's office doorway.* "You ok?"

"Yes, I am." Startled, she wiped a lone tear that was rolling down her cheek. "Um, I'm leaving for a bit call my cell if you need anything." She stood to leave and reached for her purse.

"But wait, you have new clients coming in."

"Well, you handle it for me, I can't stay!" Her voice was cracking, she was on the brink of crying.

"No problem." Ronnie recognized the weakness in Julia's voice and felt bad for her. "I'll take care of it."

Julia grabbed her purse and keys, locked her office door and left. She roamed around aimlessly ending back in her office parking lot. Her cell phone rang, it was Thomas.

"Did you forget me?" The cheerful sound of his voice was soothing. Julia stopped in her tracks.

"Oh, no, I'm on my way." She wasn't, she had forgotten and was headed home to bed.

They arrive at the same time and were able to walk in together. Julia resisted the urge to valet park but glared at the valet station longing for her life back. She valet parked anyway. She coolly went inside shaking her feeling of self-pity. Once seated, she exhaled. Thomas had a wonderful sense of humor. He could cheer up even the most solemn person. He started right in on her too. He told story after story of his college adventures. Julia laughed until her stomach ached.

After her second caramel apple martini, she requested coffee from the waiter. She shared with Thomas a decision she had made to close both the southwest office and the east office. She had made peace with the 85% decrease in agent sponsorships and was fully aware of the impact that loss of revenue had on the company as a whole. Closing the offices would mean job loss for over 20 employees whose families would also share in the devastation of the crashed real estate market.

"Julia let me help you." Julia opened her mouth but he spoke again before she could get a word out. He put his finger up. "Wait, just hear me out. If you need money for anything, I can't do a lot, but, I am sure I can help a in some way."

"Really?" She was genuinely thankful for his offer. "Thanks, but, my business is failing, this industry is crashing. I'm failing and I can't ask you to try to save me Tommy."

"Maybe I can help you to not fail." *He leaned in and touched her hand.* "I will try hard to find some business for you through my colleagues. You always support me and send me referrals and because of your referrals, I found a good level of success." *He looked at his watch and shook his head.* "I've got to get home, let's go. We will talk soon." *He paid the check then and stood up and motioned her from the booth.* "By the way Jules, I do have a few estate cases I'm working on, maybe there will be some real estate involved and you can list them if so. I will at least promise to send them your way. Ok?"

"Ok, that's fine. I will definitely accept that offer! Thanks, you're a real friend." She smiled at him warmly in appreciation of their friendship.

They left the restaurant, and as she drove home, Julia prayed for something to happen by the time she needed it to. The radio blasted announcements of several lenders closing their doors. Tears filled her eyes and flowed freely from her eyes to her cheeks. It indeed got worse before it got better.

Greedy Ass Blind Date

Julia got home and rid herself of all of her clothes. She decided to lay back and relax after having met with Thomas for drinks. She was sitting in her girlfriends' room wearing a tiny pink Vicky tank and tiny sleep shorts, watching TV. This room was her special retreat for when she needed total peace away from the world. Julia had converted a room into this "girlfriends" room and decorated it everything girlie. The walls were covered with beautiful artworks of dresses and shoes. Spread about the room was miniature collectable shoes and purses. Julia was very proud of the fine fabrics she had selected for the décor. No matter how the day went, peace would be had every time she stepped into this room.

She took a hot bath and had just laid back on the soft plushness of her fluffy fur fabric drenched chaise lounge when she heard the sound of her doorbell ringing. She thought *"who the hell is it now!"* Boy was she full of visitors lately. She didn't usually get many visitors. She rose to get to the door, figuring it was one of her sisters. Oh shit! It was Blondie her cousin. Damn! They were going on a double date at 9:00pm tonight. Julia had forgotten it was for tonight. Blondie had set Julia up with an ex-professional football player who was friends with some guy Blondie was dating. Blondie is her nick name. Her real name is Mary. That's also Julia's sister's name. Julia had nicknamed her Blondie to keep their names straight. She hated when she said Mary and everyone asked which one.

She slowly walked to the front door.

"Who is it?"

"Me girl! Open the damn door!" It was Blondie.

"Girl I completely forg--" As she opened the door Blondie cut her off.

"Hell naw! No no no! You are not getting out of this one. Girl I went through a lot to set this up."

"I'm so tired though." Julia was exhausted.

"Come on, you always cancelling shit! Just throw some jeans on and come on. Looks like you had a shower already anyways. Come, let's get out. We don't have to stay long girl."

"Damn it! I know one thing (*headed to her bedroom with Blondie following her*) he'd better be cute, trick!" (*Laughing*)

Julia pulled out a blouse and jeans and a pair of heels. She analyzed it while Blondie encouraged her it's a good outfit. She grabbed earrings, a scarf, and bracelet with watch. She removed her robe and began to quickly dress. She talked to Blondie while dressing.

"Yeah girl, he previously played for someone. Still has money, drives a big body Benz, and lives in Greatwood. He always smells nice and looks good. Seriously, he's a good one. I know you gone like him girl."

"Girl" *Julia said with a doubtful look on her face* "I've been through the ringer with dates lately. You wouldn't believe I almost got with Mitch." She busted out laughing just saying his name.

"Uhn uhn! No! Really? Girl his ass is fine as hell to me. No, you gotta tell me everything." Blondie couldn't contain her joy for hearing juicy gossip.

"He's alright, I guess." She shrugged an I-guess-so-shoulder at Blondie's comment then laughed. "Let's just say nothing happened. Girl I brought him home and he tried to get him some without a condom saying he trust me! I was like, yeah? Well, I don't trust you! I put him out. Fast!"

"What!" (*Laughing hard choking*) You actually put him out? That's hilarious! Damn! So did yall almost do it then he didn't have one or what?"

"NAKED! (*Julia emphasized her distaste for Mitch's actions*) "Hear me? We were totally naked! His dumb ass slapped my titty! Hard!"

"What! Why the hell did he slap your tit?" Blondie laughed.

"Who knows? So how do I look?" Julia did a full 180 twirl.

"Fabulous! Let's roll out."

"Hey, he better not be on no bullshit!" Julia rolled her eyes.

"Chill Jules, he's cool. Come on." Blondie smiled and rolled her eyes.

They arrived at Dave and Busters. They went to the bar but the guys were not there yet. Blondie called Ray, her date, to see how far away they were.

"They're a few minutes out. Let's get drinks."

"Ok, but damn it's so loud in here. How are we going to be able to hear each other? Who picked this place for a first date anyway?"

"Ok, (*as she gave Julia a mean look*), let's get drinks. Come on girl, try to relax and have fun. Geez!"

Julia was looking around examining the room. The bartender came over to them and took their drink order. The guys walked up while Julia was taking in the ambiance. She realized their presence when Blondie stood to greet them.

"Hey you!" Blondie said as she kissed Raymond then looked over at the other guy. "Hey Stanley. This is Julia, Julia Whitney my cousin. Julia this is Raymond my guy and his best friend Stanley."

Ray hugged Blondie then shook Julia's hand. Stanley walked to Julia and hugged her. Julia was taken aback with the hug but hugged him anyway. She quickly gave him the old head-to-toe, the one where a woman looks a man over completely in under 30 seconds. She examined that he had clean manicured hands, polished Kenneth Cole shoes, nice expensive designer jeans, and a crisp white button down shirt. He smelled of Armani Exchange cologne and didn't wear a wedding ring. She was moderately impressed with his broad shoulders; yes he was built like a football player. She tried not to crotch-watch but let's be honest what woman didn't check out the man's crotch. He seemed to be packing. She saw beautiful dark brown eyes and the darkest longest eyelashes she'd ever seen on a man. He was gorgeous. His hug felt safe and warm and she almost melted when he let her go. Not bad for a blind date. So far so good.

"Damn Mary, she's prettier than you said. How are you Julia?"

"Thank you Stanley. I'm great. You?" Julia gave him a polite smile.

"Cool. Let's sit down. I see you ladies got drinks already. Let's grab a table."

"Excuse me, (*Blondie motioned for the bartender*) Excuse me, can we take these drinks over to a table?"

"Sure, but you have to close out here. It'll be $16" He handed Blondie a printed bill for their two drinks.

"We'll grab the table." Ray tapped Stanley on the arm and walked towards the tables.

"Hey! So we have to pay for our own drinks? I smell a rat!" Julia's eyes widened and had the craziest look on her face. It was a grave insult for two men to walk away while a check was being settled.

"Shhh! Don't worry about it. He's not like that! Don't overreact." *(Blondie handed the bartender a $20 bill and grabbed her drink and Julia's)* Here, take your drink. Oh, there they are over there." She pointed towards the guys and went towards them.

"Bout time, (Ray extended his arms out to Blondie) come on over here next to me baby. Oh, I been so busy all day, it's good to see you baby." He kissed her on her cheek and cuddled her.

"Right here Julia." Stanley was standing to let Julia sit on the inside of the booth. "So, how was your day?"

"It was ok, I mostly worked from home and relaxed. Long week. How about yours?" Julia tried hard to relax.

"Umm, it was boring, not much going on at all." Stanley tried to soothe Julia.

"So what do you do? Blondie, oh I mean Mary told me you played pro ball? For who?" Julia asked politely, deciding to at least give this her full attention.

"Yes, but it's a sore subject for me; I don't like to talk about it. But now I just kind of invest in different things. Let's change the subject." Stanley was elusive.

Julia sipped her drink a few times. She could tell she just went from first class to coach with this date. It would be downhill from here.

"You guys want a drink." Blondie was super excited for some Reason. Then again she was always excited in the presence of a man. "There's a waiter. Oh and I'm starved. Let's get something to munch on."

She signaled for the waiter. Just as the waiter arrived the guys got up. The look on Julia's face was priceless. If looks could kill, her eyes could pierce their chests like bullets rushing from the barrel of an automatic weapon. Boom boom boom and dead.

"Hey we will be right back." Ray and Stanley rushed away like fire was behind them, again.

"Y'all want food? I can order for you." Blondie called after them in a very obvious and desperate plea. She knew Julia wasn't going to let this one slide by.

"No, I'm not hungry." Both men replied, almost at the same time. Julia wondered if they had rehearsed this! Was there a camera somewhere filming them? Would Ashton pop out from behind the bar?

"Well, no, we ate already." In a failed attempt to clean up his rapidly falling image, Ray stuttered as the words slid off his tongue. "We had a very late lunch. Go ahead though. Order. We'll be right back."

"What the absolute hell!" Julia stared in disbelief as they walked off. "What the hell was that all about? Why are they so damn strange! I'm ready to get out of here, now!"

"Come on Julia, they are just not hungry! No big deal. What do you want?" She turned her focus to the menu.

"Well, (*looking even more annoyed*), I'll have the fish, small Caesar side salad and a baked potato all the way no bacon. What are you having?"

"Ok, give me the steak and baked potato all the way and a small salad."

"Salad dressing?"

"Light vinaigrette please."

"Will that be all ladies?"

"Yes." Blondie and Julia replied at the same time.

Julia watched the waiter walk away then looked to Blondie. She remained quiet though. She thought about all the random guys Blondie had dated and how she had disaster after disaster. Her relationships were always full of disappointment. She had been basically bullied into entertaining this loser tonight so that Blondie could score points with this Ray person who Julia had a bad feeling about.

"So, Ray, what does he do?" Julia knew Blondie would be defensive.

"Look don't start. I know you're not hitting it off with Stanley. That's fine. But, don't start attacking my relationship with Ray. He's a good man."

The waiter brought their food. They sat in silence music blaring in the background. The sounds of games and laughter was all around. The air filled with the tender aroma of chicken fingers, ribs, bake potatoes, french fries, and every other staple the place serves.

"Hmmm, this potato is awesome. Perfect. How's your food Blondie?" She knew Blondie was still ticked at her.

"It's great girl. I'm sitting here focused on where the hell our dates are."

"Oh, yeah them. Well, I was enjoying the peace."

"Ha ha ha! Love your sarcasm Julia." She smiled wryly.

"I'm sorry. Seriously, you think they may have left?"

"Ha! No way! Leave you two lovely ladies." Ray joked as he placed his arms around Blondie. "Not a chance. We shot a game of pool. Sorry it took so long. It took longer than I thought to whoop that ass this time."

"Yeah right" Stanley chimed in. "As usual, I had to teach this dude how to play like a man." Man banter. Both men laughed. Julia was not at all amused.

"Glad you're enjoying yourselves." Blondie smiled at them, relieved that Julia was not right about them leaving. "It's fine. Hey, sure you're not hungry? The food is delish!"

Julia put her fork down and rested her back against the booth and exhaled. She couldn't finish her food.

"Wow! This is so good. They give you so much food. Whewwww."

"Oh so you're full huh?" Stanley scooted in closer to her.

"They seriously give a lot of food for one person. Who could eat all this?" As she laughed, Julia pushed her plate back and turned her fork down.

Stanley reached over to Julia's fork. He picked it up and dug deeply into her potato and ate right from her plate. Julia's mouth fell open and she gasped.

"Ummmmm good! You're right this is great. Wow. Man you gotta try this." Stanley moaned as he looked at Ray.

"What the hell! Did you really eat from my plate! Why would you do that!" Julia was pissed. "You're eating with my fork!"

"Whoa, calm down. I thought you were done?"

"But it's my food!"

"Damn! My bad, you said it was too much food!"

"No! I said it was a lot of food! Not too much! Why would you eat off of my fork anyway? You don't know me like that!"

"Look, I'm sorry, here's your fork." Stanley handed Julia her the fork but she refused.

"Oh nooooo! Hell no! You can have it now! Keep it!"

Stanley reached over and slid her plate in front of him. He proceeded to eat every drop of her food and he even ate the skin of the potato. Julia watched in disgust and shock. Mary looked in despair and knew this night was over. Ray sat watching as he toggled his view between Julia and Mary.

The waiter returned and asked if everything was alright. Stanley asked for a glass of water. The waitress left and returned with the water. Blondie asked for the check. The waitress left the black folder with the check in it. Stanley stood, drank the water in one gulp and excused himself and went to the restroom. Ray went with him.

"Look" Julia was about to let Stanley have it.

"Oh girl don't you worry", Blondie cut Julia off. "Oh don't worry, we're out of here."

"So Mary you see how every time it comes time to order food or pay for something their asses bail out! Girl get rid of this loser and find a man who knows how to date! This is awful! I really am disgusted. This is the worse date ever!"

"I agree. Well, lesson learned. He won't be getting no ass tonight from me that's for sure! Let's go." She put her credit card in the folder.

As they walk from the table, the guys returned. Blondie told Ray that she had to be somewhere else and would call him later. Stanley had a smug look on his face as he approached Julia who went and stood alone near the bar area.

"So, I guess I kind of pissed you off huh?"
"You ate my damn food! The food I paid for!"
"Can I get your number? Make it up to you?"
"No, not a chance!" Arms crossed, furious.
"Fuck you then! Your loss bitch! See ya!"

Ray walked over and extended his hand to shake Julia's who was frozen with shock. Had he just called her a bitch?

"Nice to meet you. Hope to see you again."
"Good night Ray." She rolled her eyes at him, arms folded

Ray and Stanley walked to the exit doors. They looked back, waved and left. Blondie laughed. Julia turned her nose up.

"Damn girl, he ate your damn food."
"Right!" She *laughed.* "Damn! He was a hungry son of a bitch right!" They both laughed hard happy and relieved that date was over.

Julia walked towards the door and Blondie grabbed her arm to stop her. She coerced her towards the bar.

"Hey, let's have a soda or something. I have a couple of friends in the area; we can hang with them for a bit."

"Ok, who?"

"A couple of good friends who won't eat your food! Seriously, they're cool peeps. No strings. No date. Just hanging. Cool?"

"Ok, can't get much worse." Julia smiled and motioned for the bartender.

Blondie and Julia sat at the bar and ordered cranberry juice with lime, one of Julia's favorite drinks. They laughed about the night they had and waited for Blondie's friends. The two guys showed up and they all had an enjoyable time.

After Blondie left from dropping Julia off, Julia jumped in the bed tired from a long day. As she reached her deep sleep, her phone rang. It was Thomas. He said he had the deal of a life time and she would be saved from everything she was going through and that he needed her to meet new clients at her office at 9am sharp the next day. He was brief but said he'd be there personally with these gentlemen he wanted her to meet. Julia told him she'd be there with bells on. Now she really couldn't sleep. She wondered just what kind of deal he spoke of. Eventually, she smiled feeling hopeful and drifted off to sleep like a baby.

The Meeting

Julia arrived to work early. Again, she was earlier than Ronnie. She knew she had to write last checks for the closing offices. She was saddened but, Julia hoped this meeting Thomas had set up was everything he said it would be. She was trying not to be too excited, but was filled with hope.

Promptly at 9 am, Ronnie buzzed her to let her know Thomas and two gentlemen had arrived. Ronnie brought them in. Before she left, Ronnie offered cold bottled water and coffee to the men. She returned in minutes with coffee and disappeared again. They did their introductions and took their seats. The men were both sharply dressed in black suits. Julia assessed they're designer suits and expensive shoes. She always noticed how people were dressed. Her dad told her how to read people based on the way they dressed and their shoes. The room filled with different colognes.

The first guy Maurice Richard, Julia immediately didn't like him. He looked too slick, untrustworthy. She never trusted men who smiled when nothing was said or done to smile about. He made her uneasy when he looked at her. She shook his hand and quickly withdrew from contact. He recited his resume in a boastful manner. She was appalled. She extended her hand to the second gentleman, Kevin Jones. Now this guy didn't look like your typical business man, he was well dressed, but hadn't buttoned his shirt all the way up and didn't wear a tie. He was quiet when he should be and spoke when needed. She liked him. Kevin Jones looked more like he stepped out of a magazine ad than an office building. Oh my God he was good looking. He was more "sexy" than "business" even with the suit and shoes, the shirt didn't even require cufflinks and it was amazing. He wore just a white shirt, slacks, and jacket. His shirt was unbuttoned far too low for business. But at least he was quiet and professional. Another reason to love real estate was the hot guys you got to look at. Though she didn't ever date them, it sure was nice to look at them. When their hands met, she could feel the heat. Hmm, she thought, boy is there an attraction here! He was reserved and she could tell he too felt the chemistry between them. She wanted to know more about him since he didn't recite his resume like Maurice did. She curbed her appetite to flirt. This business brought on a lot of flirting, innocent flirting, sometimes it was innocent.

"Ok, Julia, these are the gentlemen I spoke to you about. Here's the deal. I am working on an estate case and the person who retained me owns some property jointly with his deceased wife. We are settling her estate and Kevin is his representative. Maurice here, (Thomas pointed to Maurice), is a loan officer who has a client who seeks to purchase the property. This is a jumbo loan situation and requires experience. When they told me the challenges with interviewing and securing a broker for the seller, I thought of you. This gentleman is liquidating all of his assets as a result of the tragic loss of his wife and son. He will only work with a broker even though I could facilitate this purchase, which works in your favor Julia, since new business wouldn't hurt. The property in question is worth over $150 million but he will sell it for $100 million which will leave good equity even in this market."

"He's paying 7% commission and $100k btsa if collectively we can have him liquidated and this transaction closed in 90 days. Sounds too good to be true, but, his loss is our gain."

"I have a buyer who wants it for the $100 million but will need to close a different sale in order to fund this one. He later wants to finance it in hopes of pulling out his cash-in and some equity. That's it." Maurice's talked very fast and didn't make much sense at some points while he spoke.

"This seller is very picky." Thomas looked indifferently towards Maurice for interjecting. "The seller will only work with a seasoned broker, he specified a female broker, no agents. We don't know why. Anyhow, I chose you, sent him your bio and here we are. He wants to meet you tomorrow at 1pm."

Julia could quickly do math on any commission amount. Damn! Million!!! No, oh my, $8 million for a deal already in place. She was excited but kept silent while the guys spoke. She was itching to shout out "$8 million!!!! Ooohweee!!!" Wait. What's the catch? What the hell kind of deal is this? A perfect deal? Maybe it's a scam. Oh my, one of those deals in the newspapers. She turned to Thomas.

"Ok, Thomas, level with me. There are 4 people in this room. Only one is licensed in real estate, except of course you being an attorney. How exactly do these (waiving her hand in the direction of Maurice and Kevin) two gentlemen get paid. I'm sure no one works for free or just to give me a referral."

"Julia of course I earn revenue for my legal fees, they get paid from their buyers and sellers respectively. They have no other interest in the money derived from this deal. Maurice does the loan and earns a mortgage commission from that and Kevin works directly for the seller in some capacity so--"

"Look guys, as he cut Thomas off, I don't mind receiving a

referral fee if she'd like." Maurice's laugh belled out from the pit of his belly like a bronchial attack. He sounded so ignorant. Kevin jabbed him with his elbow.

"No referral fees ma'am." Kevin looked angrily at Maurice who smirked and shrugged his shoulders.

"That tells me nothing!" Julia rolled her eyes *at* Maurice after careful restraint. "No offense group, I need to know that this is a good deal solid and above the ground. Though a commission of any kind or amount sounds good right about now in this real estate climate, I'm not risking my freedom for it. Is there anything in this transaction that's going to put me, my company, or my license at risk?"

"Look!" Maurice spoke in a hostile tone towards Julia. What the hell are you trying to say? There are thousands of realtors waiting for and begging for business! What the hell--"

"Maurice wait!" Kevin placed his hands on Maurice's chest to calm him down. He spoke calmly while keeping his eyes on Julia. "Julia seriously, in a volatile state like this, surely you don't suggest we'd put ourselves or you at risk? My partner is aware of his financial obligations to me." He oozed sexiness "I receive 5% of any deal I oversee and consummate on his behalf. He trusts me and trusts my judgment. He lost his wife and son in a tragic accident and blames himself. He cannot continue his life as is and feels it beneficial to liquidate his assets. He is a billionaire and if you've ever dealt with one, they're pretty particular and sometimes eccentric. The grief he's suffered is crippling. I was best friends with his son and I too am suffering. I've worked with this family all my life. He parted ways with his previous broker for reasons unknown to me. That's it. Shall we do business or should our search continue?"

"I apologize (Thomas checked his ringing phone) I have to take this call. Be right back." He excused himself to take the call.

Thomas looked worried as Julia watched him leave the room to take his call. Judging by the look on Julia's face, this may not be what she needs. This Kevin guy is very charming, Julia thought as she returned her attention to him. I should still be leery of him. That Maurice is a handful; definitely don't want to work with him. I need this money, guess I will at least meet Mr. Money Bags and judge for myself.

"Ok, I'll need to run comps, pull title, etc., appraisal needs to be ordered, etc."

"Here *(Kevin reached into his briefcase and handed her an envelope)* I've taken the liberty of gathering comps, appraisal, and title. We will need the contract, listing agreement, survey, and must close in 90 days or less. That's the time offered per the seller. Will that be a problem?"

"No not as far as the cash portion of the sale, no. The buyer needs to understand that for his loan or whatever you guys do, it may take a while banks are not friendly right now and..."

"You won't be a part of that portion of the transaction. Just do your part!" Maurice snapped at Julia.

"Thanks Julia" Kevin cut in and gave Maurice a dirty look. "We will bear that in mind. Don't worry, Maurice is harmless. His bark is worse than his bite. We're working on his table manners. The buyer is gathering the resources for this deal, I must caution you that it is a partial cash deal. This buyer will put 75% down and the remainder is to be financed. We do have open title already."

"Next time put a leash and muzzle on him!" Julia smiled coolly at Maurice who smiled back just as coolly. "Fair enough.

I'll do all that I can. I'll need your card so that I can reach you for the meeting. Also, I need the owners' info too. As far as the loan, he *(pointing at Maurice),* only has to do his job and I don't foresee a problem, especially with that kind of cash down."

"Everything you need is in that package." Kevin pointed to the envelope laying on her desk. "Send me the contract asap and other documents and I will set up the meeting."

"Oh no, let me explain how this is going to go. I need to deal directly with the seller when it comes to the listing documents. He has to sign my representation agreement etc. and I need to explain how this process will go directly to him."

"Geez." Kevin was frustrated with Julia's intent on sticking to procedure

"Slow down Julia. I am going to put you in touch with him. Just get the paperwork together. We'll meet Fontana tomorrow, 1 pm. My assistant will send the details over. FYI…Mr. Fontana still has to agree to work with YOU."

"Wait, so is this some kind of game to you? Am I auditioning? My time is very valuable! I don't chase clients, Kevin."

"Stay with me Julia. Look, he keeps turning down realtor after realtor. I am not sure why, but, after going through 18 agents, I think he may like you. You have a tough attitude, maybe you guys will hit it off. *(Laughter)* Seriously, what do you have to lose? I'll pay you $1500 for your time if he doesn't agree to work with you. Are we good?" He extended his hand to her.

"For now we are. I'll take you at your word Mr. Jones. Thank you." Julia stood and took his hand. He lingered a bit and pulled away slowly. "Until tomorrow then."

Maurice turned his nose up and walked out just as Thomas strolled in. He smiled as entered realizing their hand shake meant they're moving forward. He gave Julia a big hug.

"Smells like you got a deal! How'd it go? Sorry I had to take that." Thomas smirked.

"Ugh!!!!!!" Julia was exasperated.

"Calm down slugger!" Laughing. "Damn! Thought you were going to rip that Maurice guy's head off!"

"I don't like him! I smell a rat. I'll deal with Kevin, not him though. Ugh! He gets under my skin!"

"Ok, I'll see what I can do to keep him away. What'd he do while I was gone?"

"Annoy the hell out of me!" She burst out laughing.

They hugged and Julia said thanks and Thomas left. She sat at her desk exasperated, then began to work on the details of this new deal. Ninety days? Cash buyer? Wow! She thumbed through the file Kevin prepared and began to comb through the appraisal and other documents. She read a typed report about Mr. Fontana.

"Billionaire Richard Fontana recently lost his wife and son on a cruise. She was his second wife of 25 years and step mother to his only son Richard Fontana Jr. They had gone on a 9 day Caribbean cruise. Mrs. Fontana had a love for water sports and was water skiing off the coast as she often indulged. She had suddenly fallen overboard the ski boat and Richard Jr. reportedly went in after her. His body was never recovered but hers washed up in a marina 2 days later. Searchers looked and looked for young Richard, but never recovered a body. He was later pronounced "assumed dead" leaving Mr. Fontana devastated."

His only son and his beloved wife of 25 years, were both gone. Richard Jr. had been eager to please his dad. He wanted to succeed his father as CEO of the family business. His dad allowed him to oversee a project of his own which ended badly costing the company 6 million dollars in losses. He was smart but far too hotheaded. Overly eager to rush into decision making without proper research or follow through. After this project failed, Richard Sr. revoked his son's rights and his position in the company. Sent him back to lower management and told him he'd have to work his way up the ladder like everyone else.

He paid him less than his own employees because he wanted him to work for promotions. He'd hoped to build his son's management skills and negotiating skills as well. Mr. Fontana was livid about the financial loss. Now, however, no loss would compare to this loss. He wanted to simply close this deal fast even if it meant taking a loss. He needed this final closure so that he too could rest in peace.

He Came Into My Life

"Good Morning Julia, this is Kevin Jones."

"Good morning, how are you?"

"I'm great! You? Are you busy?"

"I'm fantastic! Just finished a run, headed to the office."

"Same here, I hoped you could meet me at my office around 10 where we could meet before the meeting at 1pm. Go over a few things."

"Ummm, I guess. I think I can swing that, I'll need to check my schedule, make sure nothing conflicts."

"Great! Let me know. We can do lunch before the meeting as well. Is that cool?"

"Oh, I guess that will be ok." She was taken aback.

"There's a Pappadeaux near my office will that be ok?"

"Yes that's fine, hadn't been there in a while."

"I hope you can, I have some other business I hope to discuss too. I'll be on my best behavior." Kevin chuckled as he tried to lighten the mood, feeling her reluctance.

"Welllllll, ok how could I pass up a free lunch?" She chuckled as well.

"Hahaha! As if you need anyone to buy you lunch. Ok, see you then, I hope."

Julia hung up the phone and immediately called Ronnie to see if she had anything that would prohibit her from meeting Kevin at his office. Ronnie confirmed that Julia's schedule was all clear. She further voiced to Julia that she had hardly any work to do and that the phones were very quiet. Julia told Ronnie to be patient and to keep working. She assured her that things would pick up and that she'd be out all day. They hung up and Julia's attention went back to Kevin Jones. What was his deal? She was curious about the Fontana deal but also the "other" business he mentioned. Were things finally looking up for her? She drove along thinking about his comment on her not needing anyone to buy her lunch. She laughed and thought if he only knew. She resolved to make sure no one knew her financial state and that she appeared more than well positioned. When people smelled financial stress, they lost respect for you. She was becoming a very good actress.

Julia met Kevin at his office. It was extravagantly decorated. Not like she would have thought for him. He seemed more urban, low key. This place was impeccable. He presented her with a few more real estate deals representing buyers. She saw them as small deals but felt she couldn't be too choosy! She needed everything she could get. They sat and talked for a while. She enjoyed listening to him talk. He had such energy. His lips were captivating. Beautiful white teeth, probably never had a single cavity in all of his life. His hair was cut low close to the scalp. It looked soft and clean. He smelled so yummy. His hands were clean and manicured. His skin was golden brown, flawless. She liked that too. When he laughed, you could feel his whole being enjoy the moment. She wondered how his feet looked. Probably just as flawless. She caught her breath and shook off the temptation to breathe him in. Get back to business Julia! She told herself. After the meeting, she agreed to meet him at the Pappadeaux down the street. She didn't care for Pappadeaux, well, she liked it, but it was never her first choice for lunch or dinner. Black people idolize Pappadeaux too much for Julia's taste. She felt it was their way of feeling like they were going to a fancy restaurant. Many just didn't know that there is so much more out there than just a trip to Pappadeaux. He called her while she was in route but to his disappointment, she was at a nearby store. He asked her would she be long, she tried to hurry up. After 15 minutes he called again. He was not pleased that she had him waiting. He actually sounded pissed. His voice was full of tension.

"Ok Ms. Julia! I'm not accustomed to waiting for females. Might I remind you that I'm chasing your business not your ass. How long will you be, I'd hate to leave!"

"Pulling in now. I'll ignore that last remark!" She hung up sharply.

She walked in and scoped the place out. He was, sitting in the bar area, having a lemonade it seemed. He looked delicious as he sat there oblivious to her arrival, still no tie and shirt buttoned low. She pranced over to the table and sat graciously. She apologized for the delay. When he looked at her, she knew he felt the heated chemistry between them. They talked more business. He mapped out a course of action for the deals he had referred to her. They talked, laughed and ordered their meals. Julia had the chicken Caesar salad and he had a grilled blackened Opelousas. The food was impeccable. Pappas never disappoints.

They talked right up to about 30 minutes before their meeting with the seller. Julia was very relaxed and excited to have a peaceful meal which potentially will earn her closed deals. He motioned the waiter for the check, paid cash and he rose from the table. He extended his hand to Julia to escort her out. His touch was magical. Skin so soft as if he'd never did a hard day's work in all his years on earth. He was strong and led her with kind force from the restaurant. He was in charge. He knew it too. She wondered why the hell she was feeling magic! This guy was definitely off limits and she shouldn't be looking let alone buying into magic. Over the course of the next few weeks this view would change.

They arrived at Mr. Fontana's office on Post Oak in one of the most exquisite pieces of commercial property in town. She followed his car into the parking garage. Once inside a voluptuous receptionist greeted him in the most purposeful flirt she could muster up. She was about 5'1, huge breast and a very cute face. Her hair was curly and dark. She was a perky super bubbly people pleaser. She didn't seem very bright, but Julia imagined she was pretty smart to be able to be the voice and face visitors would hear and see first. He down played the attention she gave him and signaled Julia to sit. He walked over to the receptionist and whispered so softly that Julia couldn't hear his words clearly. Then he joined Julia and took a seat.

His phone rang and he told Julia he had to leave. She looked alarmed and stood, moved close to him. She leaned in close to him.

"Must you go? Won't you at least introduce us?" Julia whispered. "Besides you said we'd go by the property, don't you have to escort me there?"

"Sorry, I really have to go or else I would stay. I think it will be fine to go by the house at another time. I'll take you early next week. Give him my regards."

Kevin left. The receptionist called out to Julia, who was still watching Kevin as he boarded the elevator.

"Ms. Whitney, Mr. Fontana will see you now. Follow me."

Julia followed her down a long hallway through amazing glass doors. She pointed her hands to the only door past the glass doors which had the single word "Fontana" on it. Voluptuous tapped lightly then opened the door and walked Julia in. She announced Julia and swiftly marched out of sight.

Julia looked nervously over the room, filled with golf trophies, sporting event paraphernalia, and everything "man" throughout. It was an amazing view and totally enclosed in delicate glass windows. Mr. Fontana had his back to the door and slowly turned his chair to face Julia. He was a beautiful older man well put together and immaculately dressed in everything custom. His cufflinks alone must have cost a mortgage payment. His skin had aged gracefully, he didn't look his age at all. She knew that a man his age kept himself well put together as a result of god living and lots of money. His aged skin was still just as flawless as a man half his age. It was a fight for most women but men with money tend to have great skin.

She walked over to his desk and extended her hand to shake his. He rose to shake her hand.

"Hello Mr. Fontana, I'm Julia Whitney, which you already know. How are you sir" *Why the hell am I nervous?*

"As well as can be considering I've just buried my wife and son. Call me Richard please."

"I am so sorry sir *(flushed with embarrassment)* I was being polite. I'm so sorry for your loss and wish I could do something, anything to ease your pain, but I know no one can."

"Thank you dear." He motioned for her hand and shook it while covering hers with his other hand. "Thank you child. I know, I'm sorry; I need to come up with a better way to answer that question. I'm being an old ass." He laughed a gentle genuine laugh.

"Oh that's fine. It did catch me off guard." She felt relieved.

"Please sit. Can I offer you a drink? Coffee or water, bourbon?"

"No, thank you. Maybe water later but let's get right to it if you don't mind."

"I like you already. You know my situation so let's get to it."

"Thank you. Here are the documents you requested and those needed to work this deal from beginning to fruition."

"I love fruition. It is imperative that we understand each other as well. I know you're a good broker. I did some research on you."

"Research?" Julia gave him a puzzled look.

"Yes ma'am, like background check, financials, etc. Just the standard stuff. It all checks out. But I do see that you're in some trouble now financially?"

"Background check? I never authorized that! *(Insulted and overcome with anger)* What! How could you know such a thing? How dare you? What gives you the right to pry into my finances! That's private information, what is this about?" Angered beyond belief, Julia was caught off guard.

"Ma'am, calm down. Julia, I didn't mean to offend you. I have to do these checks to protect myself and make sure I know who I am trusting. This is a lot of money at stake here and I needed to know you're a woman of integrity. The information stays here. This is very standard and customary for us here."

"Ok *(taking a deep breath while trying to grab a hold of her composure, but still sulking over his indiscretion)* Richard! (*In a hardened tone*) I am in no way discussing my financials with you or anyone else for that matter. I understand that you want to protect yourself; however, I am truly offended. With that being said, let's go over the information necessary for closing this deal sir. FYI...all other areas of my life are off limits, clear?"

"I understand Julia. It's very clear" He sat up straight and a small inclination of embarrassment overcame him.

Julia went over all of the paperwork. Richard reviewed it and willingly signed the documents. He stood and shook her hand. She moved towards his office door and he stopped her.

"Come with me a second."
"Why?" Julia was concerned.
"Please"
"Ok, I have another appointment soon."

He took her into a small room that she knew was a break room. He was very serious about this impromptu move to this room. It was smaller than a typical break room. There was a small college size refrigerator and microwave, a small round table with 3 chairs, and a wall of cabinets alongside the far wall. The walls were bare and it appeared this room was a project started but never finished. He motioned her to enter first and he closed the door behind them.

"Julia, I apologize for catching you off guard with the background situation. I need to trust you. I have to be able to trust you. Do you abide by the rules of your license? Where you have to keep everything that we speak of confidential like you said?"

Julia looked at the desperacy in his eyes and she grew concerned. He held her hand almost pleading with her for some undisclosed help. This mans distress went beyond the loss of his family.

"Yes of course. I'd die before I would betray any client. Why? Is everything ok with this deal? Are you ok? Is there something I should know?"

"That's all I needed to know. Everything's just fine. My assistant will need copies of those documents. You can have them copied on your way out. I appreciate your help and look forward to putting all of this to rest. We will talk soon and keep me posted as necessary." Richards's demeanor went from desperate to satisfied just that quickly.

He hurried from the room without any further explanation. Julia stood there not knowing what to think about what just happened.

"What the hell!" She watched him leave the small room in haste.

This is a weird situation. What have I gotten myself into? Please God let this thing close quickly! Once back inside of her car, Julia called Kevin.

"Jones here."

"Glad you answered. *(Annoyed by how he answered the phone)* This is Julia. I need to see the property today."

"Hello Julia. *(She could hear him chuckle)* You get right to the point huh? I apologize about earlier. I got a call from my dad, he lives in Brenham. It couldn't be helped, he needed me. He almost sounded suicidal in his request for me to come to him. I had to go. Give me 2 hours and I can show you the house."

"Fine, call me when you are ready."

"Can I pick you up?"

"Umm" She wasn't sure she wanted to be in a car with him.

"It will be easier, the house is occupied and in a gated community with armed security, and it'd be much easier if I escort you. Say yes."

"Yes, from my office."

He Talked a Good Talk

He picked her up in front of her office building. He was prompt, on time and dressed casually in jeans and a crisp black shirt with black buttons, very nice. He wore black boots which made him look kind of like a cowboy. He even had the belt buckle. He looked gorgeous to her, more so than before.

They made their way down the long and winding highway. Upon exiting, they turned sharply on a beautiful lonely road through the grandest trees which encompassed a fairy tale like neighborhood. Oddly, Julia hadn't been here before and was a bit embarrassed as she took it all in. She had prided herself on knowing every inch of Houston. They continued along this fairy tale lonely road towards a rod iron luxury gated entry to what seemed like the neighborhood they were seeking. Kevin pulled up to the armed security officer and exchanged niceties. Julia noticed that the security man was actually a full fledge law enforcement officer who manning the gates. Julia knew all of Houston but this was new to her. It was stocked full of mature trees and lush landscaping. The trees were met with such delicately beautiful flowers that they didn't even seem real. Each property was the length of an entire city block. She was definitely alert and poised to see the most expensive homes she'd ever seen. Mr. Fontana had gone on and on about how his late wife came to love this place.

When he married her she wasn't very worldly at all. It's funny how money opens your mind and exposes you to new and unheard of things. Many worried that she may be a financial opportunist. He described her as being much far from that. She was very smart; he described her as a very intelligent and kind lady. He'd shown Julia pictures of her and she looked lively and yes very pretty. You could feel the love they shared just from his kind words, words that penetrate the soul. They had the kind of love that survives death. He would have given her the world if she asked for it. It was such a sad loss.

As they moved right into the deep curve in the road, it came to a dead end at the entry of the Fontana Estate. He drove up to the gated entry which had the letters RFE engraved on them. There were cameras everywhere and two armed men approached the car but moved to either side of Kevin's car. Kevin's silence went virtually unnoticed as Julia enjoyed the view. He lowered his stereo which played softly the sweet hues of Boney James, one of her favorites. This house was priceless, literally priceless. It was so expensively built; no amount of money could be paid for it. One of those properties that was over-built for the area even in the deepest section of this luxurious neighborhood.

Julia thought this must be a castle of sorts. She envisioned coming home to a mansion like this. The long street was filled with mature oak trees that engulfed the huge mansions spanning through to the dead end. Every imaginable flower welcomed you along with the sound of nature that surrounded your car as you drove the length of this private mansion filled neighborhood. To Julia, thoughts like that were but a dream.

When they pulled up, Kevin signaled the valet to meet him and the guy did just that. Valet? Hmm, she thought. Kevin never slowed down his bright yellow Lamborghini; a car Julia didn't care for, but, Kevin's choice in vehicles. This car was such a waste of metal and far too expensive of a man toy. There's his flaw. Every man had a flaw, some were hard to detect, and Kevin drove his. She laughed inside.

The land was impeccably maintained, with mature landscaping filled with beautiful seasonal flowers. The house was staffed full of servants for the interior as well as the exterior. They even had armed guards walking the property. Julia couldn't phantom what this was all about. She asked no questions and for the first time in her life she was perfectly compliant and quiet. The elevation went on forever it was absolutely breathtaking. The interior was decorated to the tune of million dollars. It reminded her of what you'd see in a museum. Lots of tapestry, fine silks, ceiling to floor curtains, dated furniture that was of course antique. It had those old statues of great historians. It was full of history and not appetizing to Julia at all. She was more modern or contemporary.

The art was priceless collectors' editions of original works by the most famed artists. Most of the individual pieces held value at over a million dollars each. There was a great room with walls that were entirely covered with custom Italian leather. Even the bathroom was overstated with those toilets that cleanse you after you go. Julia was borderline appalled. Hours later after a tour of the grounds and every nook and cranny, too much for her to remember, Julia was exhausted. She was very overwhelmed.

This property was more that she imagined. Complete with staff quarters and private entrances for the staff, so that they didn't disturb the masters of the house. She didn't know what she thought it would be like, but it was far more than anything she could conceive. The house was complete with a basketball & tennis court, several pools, two outdoor kitchens as large as Julia's entire home, which was by no means small, an indoor pool, and an outdoor pool. The rooms all had private bathrooms, sitting areas, private balconies, and breakfast bars. Her thoughts remained focused on the fact that the servants were all live in and had their own entry and quarters. This house was awesome and yet creepy, far too much house for just two or three people.

She was amazed. Now, she could accept the price of the home and the deal as a whole. Only one thing bothered her, she knew why and who the seller was but what was the story with the buyer? They didn't have the name of the company yet, some company called "blank" Holdings or something like that. Maurice said he'd fill it in on the contract when the buyer signed it. She'd know more when they sent the contract back to her and she could send it to Mr. Fontana. What was their angle? Would they want to live in it? Who could call this home? That would have to wait. Right now she needed to take all of this in. She was happy it wasn't a traditional deal where she had to place a lockbox, yard sign, etc. She could only imagine what it would be like to locate a buyer for a home like this if placed on the open market. She didn't like that thought. It would probably take at least a year to get it sold and realistically longer than that.

"So what do you think?" He handed her a glass of wine brought over by a beautiful young servant.

"I am overwhelmed. Pleased to be here, but, I seriously didn't expect this. It's amazing."

"I know. It's pretty amazing. (Moving closer to her, enough that the heat from both their bodies connected) I'm glad you like it."

"Do you live here? You're awfully familiar with it, and it's so huge! How could you remember it all?"

"Nah. *(Mild laughter)* I don't live here, well, sometimes I do spend the night. I do spend a lot of time here and have access whenever I want. We could hang out here sometimes if you like."

"Oh *(caught off guard by that comment, she blew it off)* yeah actually, I'd very much like to leave now if we are done. I am a little tired now."

"Ok, let's go."

Kevin gulped down his last sip of wine and Julia did the same to follow suit. They headed through what seemed to be a maze and Kevin signaled the valet.

As they rode away from the house, they both rested their arms on the middle console armrest. He looked very handsome in that unbuttoned shirt. The fabric was so nice, the shirt was definitely custom, she was sure. It was so beautiful that it made her want to touch it and before she knew it, her hand caressed the fabric of his shirt collar and slightly brushed his hair line. He looked over at her. She snapped her hand back.

"I apologize, it's just such a unique fabric, I don't know why I did that, very out of line. I didn't mean anything, I swear!"

"Its ok, no big deal. Actually, I get a lot of compliments every time I wear it. It's was a gift. A year ago I went to my tailors' office; this was one of his newer fabrics. He said he hadn't been able to move it and that it took someone bold to pull it off like me. He said that about all of his new fabrics. But this one was very unique to me. It didn't look like much on the bolt to others who saw it. He threw it in with a suit I bought. I use Mr. Fontana's tailor and he's very good as you can see."

His smirk made her feel even more embarrassed and left her wondering what he was thinking. They arrived back to her car and she hopped out quickly as she said goodbye. He got out of his car and extended his hand to shake hers. She did and their hands lingered for a moment, captivated by each other's touch. Still holding hands, she thanked him for the tour and told him they'd talk soon.

Julia arrived home and she had barely closed the door when her cell phone rang. She wondered who it was now, she needed to relax and unwind. It was Kevin. He called to ask her to meet him tomorrow, business of course, tomorrow at Starbucks around 6. She agreed. They talked for 4 hours on that phone call about everything from real estate to bed linen. She found it very easy to talk to him, too easy. They arranged to meet at the Star Bucks on Post Oak and Westheimer in the Galleria area then said their goodnights and she drifted off to sleep with a smile.

Julia sat in her car, waiting for this man. Kevin Jones, 6 feet of gorgeous with connections, deals, money, sexiness. She was in the parking lot of Star Bucks nervous. Julia realized she was a bit excited to meet him, she reminded herself that this was business. He had already given her four new files. She was unsure if any of them would pan out but it was worth the try and kept Ronnie busy at the office. She reminisced about their long 4 hour conversation the night before. She liked him. He was very nice and had been through similar things as her. She was trying to end the call after she accepted his meeting proposal but he was a very forceful and leading man.

He led the conversation right from business to personal. She didn't catch it before she went there but later rethought the conversation and realized how easily he guided her from professional to personal subject matter. They had a lot in common. He went through a terrible break up and so did she. He was trying to recoup from some losses, he and his best friend had a strange parting of ways just like her and hers. They both had no kids, and loved nice things. He frequented fine restaurants and had a few he schooled her on. It was a refreshing conversation full of unacknowledged chemistry.

She concluded that he was a nice guy, respectful and not openly flirty like most men. He kept his cool and was self-confident and controlled. Oh he was something to know. She wanted to know him. She also reminded herself of the roller coaster ride she had been on. But, for some reason, she felt chemistry with him. This was different. This feeling was different. Why was she drawn to him? Willing to open up to him and allow him to know her. This was a chemistry she could end up regretting. Since he was respectful and didn't hit on her, she knew she could keep it business. Still, she remembered all the previous relationship drama she'd been through. She tried to suppress the memories of OJ, Mr. King, and not to mention her failed relationship to what's his name. She had been on a personal path of destruction ever since the breakup. She'd told herself many times lately, "It's just something to do". Her front yard was missing a whole damn tree because she was "just doing" something. What did Kevin want?

Why was he helping her? Feeding her deals? Surely he knew another agent. Maybe she was paranoid. Even though he was so sweet and helpful he seemed to have two sides. On one hand he was good, charming and kind. On the other, he came across as someone who shouldn't be crossed. He seemed shrewd. He came across as someone who was always up to something, one who always had an agenda. So what was his? She didn't know, but, the way he handled her at their lunch sure made her want to know him more. Why wasn't he chasing her ass? He wasn't at all intimidated by her. She wasn't sure but, as long as she remained in control, she saw no harm in a little hanging out and a cup of coffee with a new friend. She was developing an interest in Kevin though and tensions were about to rise even more.

He tapped on her window right about then. He startled her. She was hiding her excitement as Kevin opened her door. He really was beautiful, the Morris Chestnut beautiful. His smile was the Dwayne "the Rock" Johnson beautiful. His skin was the Boris Kudjoe beautiful. Damn! He always had his damn shirt unbuttoned! She almost told him to button it up but nah!

Her body was speaking and she was desperately ignoring its call. They walked into Starbucks and he ordered for her. She was shocked and a little impressed that he had gotten her drink right. He chuckled.

"Don't give me too much credit, I called Ronnie and asked her what you liked. She told me."
"You're right, I gave you too much credit."

She laughed, and then they laughed in unison. Julia wondered why he called Ronnie, did he really want to know what she liked or was it to make a laugh out of the situation? Who knew?

They talked for hours until Starbucks was closing. They laughed at the realization they'd been there that long. Kevin stood up and he walked her to her car. He thanked her for meeting him. She smiled and told him he's very nice company.

"Well, all good things must come to an end" He spoke as he held her hand.
"So true."
"You have your keys ready?"

"Yes, thank you for walking me to my car. See you soon." She chirped her alarm and got into her car.

"Really, How soon?" He sounded hopeful.

"Bye Kevin."

She looked back to him as she started her ignition and pulled away. She smiled at him as he stood there like a child with his "what's up" arms out. Julia smiled and so did he. His hands waved bye and she drove away.

Julia had a very nice time with him, just easy and laid back. He'd told her how he'd recently gotten a divorce. That he didn't have any kids either. He spends a lot of time with his mom and was working hard on many projects.

When she arrived at the traffic light intersecting Westheimer and the 610 Loop, Kevin rolled up alongside her, honked his horn and motioned her to let her window down. He asked her where she was going.

"Home"

"Don't go yet, let me show you something."

"Hmm, I'm a little tired, I--"

"Come on, live a little."

"Ok, what, where?"

"Follow me."

The light changed, and she followed him. He turned towards and ventured around the Post Oak area where there sat a stream of townhomes. He pulled into the back side of a group of town homes. He asked her to pull into the garage. Julia's internal alarm went off. She still followed him in.

"This is my latest conquest."

"It's lovely, you live here?"

"Yeah, since the divorce, I down sized, left the house to her. I didn't mind because I love property anyway. Look around what do you think? Think you can sell this?"

"It's lovely. Of course anything can be sold, but, yes."

"I'd like you to put it on the market for me."

"Thought you just bought it?"

"Well I've had it for a year, had a friend living here, now me. But I don't want it anymore. I need liquid; I have a lot of money tied up here and overseas. Did some risky investing and need to cash out to recoup my losses."

"Oh I see. So that's why you brought me here?"

"What did you think? I told you I'm chasing the business—"

"I know, I know, not my ass."

They both finished his sentence at the same time and laughed. He moved closer to Julia, and whispered.

"But damn Julia you're so fine! You sure make it hard!"

"Wow! *(Nervously)* I didn't see that coming."

"Sorry, honestly this is just business. Just a compliment and observation that's all." Kevin's hands surrendered innocently into the air.

"I am only interested in the business as well." She lied.

"No problem. Let's go upstairs I want to show you one more thing."

"What?"

"Don't be so scared, it's just my bedroom but not my bed ok? It will only take a second. I want you to do something with me.

Don't worry, still not chasing the ass." Smiling the come-fuck-me-smile.

"Fine." She was intrigued. She smirked while allowing him to lead her. His smile gave way that he was definitely interested in the ass as well.

She followed him upstairs. They entered the master suite, which was wonderfully oversized and absolutely breathtaking. There were high cathedral ceilings, double crown molding. It had impeccable craftsmanship, well-built and of course bachelors décor. His decor was masculine, huge king-sized bed covered in a white and chocolate duvet with lots of pillows. The choice of art was divine, even though the art rested against the wall and still had to be hung. There were lots of boxes encompassing the room. Kevin motioned her to what appeared to be a prayer corner. Kevin had lots of religious books and there on the small table sat a bible opened as if he'd just finished reading from it. He knelt before the table prompting Julia to do the same. Surprising her, he began to lead her in prayer. They prayed together.

Here we are before you Lord asking you to Bless us. We seek business blessings today and thank you in advance for showering your grace upon us. (Kevin prayed eloquently) We recognize without you nothing is possible and with you we can conquer the world. Please bless us both that we may someday find love with someone you yourself handpicked for us. We ask father for these things for the person knelt beside us today, in Jesus name. Amen.

Praying together? Julia was truly taken aback. She was taken by the fact that he was a Christian and a praying man! This was one of the most beautiful things a guy had ever done with her. She rose up at his urging. He began to walk off and pulled her along. He gave her a piece of art which was a beautiful picture in an amazing frame. It had a cream background and the two beautiful bodies of a man and woman that were entertwined so well, you had to study it to see where one body ended and the other began. The artist name was one she had never heard of and scripted in beautiful artsy penmanship. It seemed very expensive. She refused it at first, but he insisted. He was very persuasive. She took it with her.

He walked her through his home, to his garage and to her car. She used her remote to open the trunk and he placed the art in it for her. He thanked her for having a look, and asked her to let him know what she needed to list it and get it sold for him. He kneeled and leaned in to her and whispered again softly but with distinct masculinity.

"I do want you Julia, but not just the ass, the whole package. I like you. I hope you don't mind me pursuing you. Be careful on your drive home, good night." He let her hand go and did not wait for her reply.

He closed her door, smiled, walked off and she sat for minutes as he entered his home.

"How commanding! Oh how I love a take charge kinda of man! I like him and a girl loves a leading man! He's so me! This (pause) I will take my time on. (*She whispered to herself*). Hmmm, the business not the ass *(she smiled)*. Yeah, the business and the ass!"

Julia drove off determined she would not end up "just doing something" again. She decided that if he properly asked, she would actually date him. She wanted to know him and have it be more than just another "something to do". No sex!

Wine On My Lips

Six weeks into the deal closing, Julia and Kevin were inseparable. She had 2 closings bringing in just under $10,000 because of Kevin's referrals. She had his personal deal in underwriting and things looked promising. He was wooing her off her feet. They flew to New York for lunch, Los Angeles for new lingerie shopping spree, and were headed to Miami for the weekend. She hadn't noticed she was paying for more and more lunches and dinners but most of the time, he paid her back.

She lent him her atm card just the other day because he said his money was tied up in some deal and he was very short on cash. He told her he had deals being finalized that same week and would catch her up. He had not given her the card back, but did pay the money back fast. He'd been to her house all the time and rarely did she ever make it back to his house after the first visit there except to show it to buyers wanting a tour. For some unknown reason he did not want it in the multiple listing service he only wanted a yard sign out. She hated that part but he was firm on that. He set up all of the showings, there were not many. She showed it a couple of times then he did all other showings. He was particular about that part since he was still occupying it.

Julia didn't feel any adverse feelings towards how financially involved she had become with him. After all, he was buying her things and showering her with gifts. She paid for Los Angeles and Miami on her credit card, which he said he'd pay off later, but he did pay for New York. They spent quite a lot of money there, more than the other trips together. They went out all the time and ate most of their meals in restaurants. Many of which she had never been to. That was exciting for Julia.

They even went to the museum. Julia hadn't been to a museum in Houston in a long time. Tonight, the night before Miami, Julia prepared for their date.

Felt good to be on a date! An actual date with someone she genuinely cared about. They planned a romantic dinner and a play. They planned to listen to some good jazz afterwards. Kevin was good for that. They went everywhere and he knew how to have a good time. She liked him a lot. She may have been falling for him more than she thought possible. He was not what she thought. How did he know just what to say all the time? Even when he knew she wouldn't agree with him. They were dating now exclusively and still hadn't slept together. He was very much into the word of God and that was fine with her. She was comfortable with him. Kevin even had a key to her house.

She didn't actually give him a key, more like loaned it to him. One day he wanted to cook for her so she gave him the spare key that Ronnie used when she needed her to and he never returned it. He talked about marrying her one day and having kids with her. He spoke of what great parents they'd make together. Though they never had sex, they did manage to be very intimate in other ways such as kissing and the infamous grinding each other. He was from a big family and said he wanted one of his own one day. Julia didn't want to get married, even though she liked him a lot, marriage thoughts fell flat on her. She lost a lot of money in her own divorce and just couldn't bring herself to say I do again. Marriage was definitely off the table for her right now but she wouldn't dare kill his dreams if that's what he wanted. Julia was flattered he would talk about marriage. Most guys ran from it. She didn't close the door entirely on marriage; she just knew it wasn't for her right now. Her faith in God led her to believe in love. When they spoke of kids, she smiled and said maybe.

He didn't come across as the kind to settle down but she knew he could be Mr. Right, God willing.

They arrived at their favorite spot Grand Lux for dinner. His car was always immaculate, just perfect for a neat freak like Julia. He opened her door. When he opened the door she sat there unmoved.

"What? Why are you still sitting there?"

"My daddy told me to never let a man open my door unless he intends to do it always. Are you just doing this now or is this really you?"

"Oh really? Hmmm, well, I plan on doing this for life. Now will you join me inside please ma'am?"

"Ok." She warmed inside after his words or how he said those words. Ok. She smiled on the left side of her mouth then showed just enough of her pearly whites to bring him to his knees.

He took her into the restaurant, hand in hand. She ordered what she always ordered, the cedar planked salmon, steamed rice, corn and the red cabbage. She never could figure out what they did to that cabbage. It was awesome and though she is a great cook, she just couldn't mimic the cabbage.

He ordered her a caramel apple martini and had one too. She laughed inside as he ordered himself a girly drink. But knew he wasn't a drinker and was being polite and sociable. She actually loved that he wasn't a drinker. She determined men who were regular drinkers ended up being assholes. She dated a few and they proved to be real assholes. Of course she knew all men who drank were probably not assholes but oh well. They ate and shared his favorite chocolate chip cookies. They left there, went to his friends play, and later went downtown to listen to some jazz music. As they sipped wine, they enjoyed getting to further know each other over the romantic hues of soft jazz music. He stressed how much he wanted to marry her someday and he told her he really cared for her. Kevin said he'd never let her go and he would be hers forever. Again he spoke of babies and that he wanted to do all of this sooner than later. She just smiled. She even envisioned a life with him. Who knows, she thought. Maybe God sent him to her. She wasn't sure. For now she'd enjoy the relationship they have. They left the jazz bar and when they got into the car, things heated up.

"Ok, so I've waited patiently. I really want to see those tits now."

"Oh my! Straight to the point! I don't know what to say." His words sent fire right to her panties.

"Come on baby, let me have a look. Hard enough sleeping in the same bed and not getting it. Let me have a look."

Julia turned to him and pulled down her blouse from the neck line. She showed her very sumptuous "double-d" caramel breast. His mouth dropped open fast.

"Wow! Exactly what I expected! Oh yeah, I must have some of you Julia. Hell all of you!"

"Kiss them." She ordered seductively. Longing for his hot tongue to indulge her needs.

Kevin gently touched her breast then leaned in to suck each nipple. He enjoyed himself and bit gently on her nipples sending cream from her core. She grabbed his head as he consumed her breast and pulled him closer and closer. Yearning for him and craving more of him. He stopped and started the car, leaving her in sides burning.

"Don't worry, I will get you to a bed and yeah, it's on!"
"Yes! *(Breathlessly straightening her blouse)* Please, let's hurry!"

Kevin took the exit to her office.

"Where are we going? Why did you exit?"
"Your office is closer and I'd like to have you on that big desk of yours. It's all I could think of the first day I met you."
"Oh boy, really?" *Blushing.*

They entered her building kissing manically. Kevin's hands were all over her and hers all over him. She wanted to just go home but the heat and passion was overwhelming. She couldn't think straight.

They made it into her office and he took her blouse off above her head. Made his way to sucking more of her breast and his manhood hard in her hands. She held his head close as he undid her zipper. She tried to kick off her heels but he whispered a soft no, don't, leave them on. He pressed her down onto the sofa and laid on top of her. There he motioned her to spread her legs as he removed her skirt. She undid his pants and pulled them down. He kicked them to the floor. Laying on top of her he somehow had a condom in his hands and opened it. She caressed his chest hairs and slid her hands slowly over his well-worked out chest. He kissed her again and with the passion of a thousand men he took her entering her body giving her an orgasmic rush that spread throughout her entire body. He filled her so completely that she really lost her mind. He fit so perfectly inside of her; she knew this was all right. After the best orgasm ever, they made it to her house and had more wine. They sipped their drinks in her bedroom while soft music played over her intercom. He complimented her décor and told her she's the most remarkable woman he'd ever met. He stood to kiss her and whispered in her ear as he nibbled it while undressing her at the same time.

"You're pretty hard to get Julia, but damn! I've never had it easy. I'm going to conquer you and make you mines forever."

The sweetest sound she had ever heard, so romantic and gentle. He melted her heart and won her full attention, oblivious to his use of the word "conquer".

He licked every drop of the red wine off her lips and sucked every inch of her body as they made sweet passionate love all night long until neither could move. They laid naked and full of each other.

"What happened to doing it on my desk?"
"Changed my mind. Selfishly, I wanted to be the hardest thing you were on tonight."

Words on My Heart

Kevin stopped by, unannounced, to Julia's office. Ronnie didn't like him. She didn't know why but, so much as told Julia so. Julia reminded Ronnie that the big reason why she liked her so much had always been how she stayed out of her business. That let Ronnie know to back down.

Kevin brought Julia 12 beautiful white roses. After that trip to Miami, she was knee deep in work and really didn't have time to socialize. But, as usual, she stopped and went to lunch with him just as he requested. He always got his way.

They often ate at his favorite Mexican spot around the corner. It was close by her office and she could get back to work easily. When it came time to pay, he patted his chest then his pants pockets. He looked at Julia.

"Hey you got this? I'll give it back later when I get my wallet. I think I left it at home. Damn!" He was still searching for it.

"Oh sure, yeah of course." As she pulled out her Gucci wallet and handed the waiter her credit card, she seemed annoyed. He was very irresponsible with that damn wallet.

"I really apologize about that. I must have left it in my jacket at the house."

"That's fine don't worry about it. I can get it sometimes too. Really, it's not a big deal. Let's go."

Julia heard of men who used women for money. She didn't think Kevin was doing that, but sometimes she hated being placed in the "financially responsible" position though. She wasn't the kind of chick to get taken for a ride. But, sometimes she did wonder. The next day, he came to her office and left a $100 bill with Ronnie. When she got there Ronnie handed her a thank you card with the hundred dollar bill inside. Julia smiled as she read the note,

"You're safe with me, thanks for lunch.
Now I'm chasing the ass not the business"

That was a sign to her that she was safe in his hands and was not being used at all.

That night they went out to dinner and a movie. They walked around the Woodlands mall then over to the shops and by the water. It was a beautiful night out and she enjoyed sitting by the water. Julia and Kevin talked and talked. One would have thought Julia would be comfortable enough to confide in Kevin about her true financial status. She just didn't trust anyone. She had way too much pride. Kevin went on about how remarkable she is and how awesome it is to be with someone who has their stuff together. A woman who is not looking for a man to take care of them, rescue her and pay all her bills. He said it was refreshing.

Julia thought, *"Wow, wish someone would rescue me, and pay all my bills."*

She had $20,000 or more a month in bills. She was barely staying afloat. Kevin's spending and constantly intertwining her in it was costing her what she was earning. Deals were closing, but, they moved slowly. Oh well, her financial state will just be her little secret lie and when Mr. Fontana's deal closes, things will be a world better. She'll be able to pay off her house, credit cards, all her bills, and revamp her company too.

When they arrived back to her house, Kevin told her how much fun he had and that he was falling in love with her. Again, he said he could see them getting married and having kids this time next year. He wouldn't let her respond, but, kissed her on the lips which led to more good sex. He kissed her with more passion than usual and said he had an early day tomorrow and had to go home. She was surprised he was leaving. The day went to well. Why did he really leave?

Heart Seems So Cold

Everything smelled so delicious. All of the food was ready and this was expected to be an amazing party at Julia's house. Kevin said he'd be over to meet her family and hang out for the whole party. He said he had a few stops like to his mother's house and his sister's house before he'd get there.

Julia had made barbequed spare ribs and chicken wings, the best potato salad in Texas (so she thought), lasagna balls, fresh sautéed green beans, a Caesar salad, and three cheese corn casserole another one of her specialties. She made several bread choices such as jalapeno corn bread muffins, garlic bread, homemade biscuits, buttered rolls, and blueberry muffins. She was proud of her table setting covered in fine linen the colors were red white and blue, perfect for the holiday. She planned a nice firework show as well.

Julia made fresh strawberry lemonade topped with fresh blueberries. She served everything in her favorite Princess house crystal and china. Julia was a connoisseur of fine things. She wanted everything that was the best. She had spent all morning preparing her home to receive her guest. She invited her sisters, their common friends, Kevin, a few colleagues, and then she remembered, she was supposed to do all of this with her best friend or ex best friend Erica. She remembered their last words and how Erica had tried several times to call her and she just wasn't up to talking to her. She hated what happened but knew Erica was toxic. She shook her head and continued putting the final touches on everything.

Julia stepped back and looked at the lovely decorations, balloons, silver ribbons, large decorative bows and everything 4th of July. She was proud.

As the guest started to arrive, Julia's hired servers were in place poised and ready to serve drinks and appetizers. Yes, she hired servers. Things had gotten a little better for Julia financially. Kevin was feeding her a lot of business. Julia was not yet comfortable but was very optimistic about her finances. She was still in heavy debt and not out of the woods. Not the smartest idea, since she had just had a few closings, Julia had spent a lot of money on this party as well as on and with Kevin. Though things were better since she closed the other offices and she was having closings, still, things were tight and the market was tighter. Banks were not lending and she was not out of the woods.

Julia's relationship with Kevin was moving fast. He was always around and she had no breathing room. They were together so often that she hardly had time to truly look at her situation let alone her relationship with him. It was moving faster than she wanted. She was not at her best and had become weakened by this relationship. Her instincts were not polished like they usually were. Kevin was slowly breaking down all of her boundaries. He came and went as he pleased in and out of her office. He was having his meetings in her conference room. This made her uncomfortable, but, she did nothing. He promised things and sometimes he didn't deliver. When he came back around he'd act like nothing happened. Still, they were inseparable.

The guest arrived as directed, dressed in the colors of freedom, reflecting true patronage of the American flag. Julia took pictures and greeted everyone. Her good friend Ralph sang songs and she even had a comedian telling jokes as people marveled at the display of humor.

As the night wore on, Julia became concerned that a couple of hours into the party, still no Kevin. She grabbed her cell and tried to call him. No answer. Julia stood at the door, makeup still flawless and hair silky as it always was, just after her salon visit. She was striking in her white American flag t-shirt and Capri pants. Her heels were 4 inches and she walked in them like she was born to do so. There were several single men there who wanted her attention. She withdrew from their attention and smiled politely. Julia's sister, Mary, asked her where Kevin was and Julia shook her head in embarrassment. She had no idea. She was embarrassed and hurt. She told her sister he was caught up at his family's house and would make it if he can. Mary looked warily after Julia as she walked away. Mary was worried about Julia. Mary felt Julia was always covering for Kevin but she didn't know why.

After the last guest left, Julia assisted the servers with the cleanup detail. She was very particular about cleanliness and décor. She wanted everything put in its place. She was obsessive compulsive. The lead server was growing frustrated with Julia. She snapped at Julia when Julia asked her to wipe a piece of crystal for a second time. Julia saw water spots and wanted them gone. The server pretended not to see them. Julia asked her if it would be ok for her to pay her half the bill since she was rendering half the service. The other servers chuckled while the lead server went on and wiped the crystal again. Julia paid them the balance and escorted them to her back door.

She quickly went to her cell phone to see if Kevin had called her back. No missed calls were in her call log. Julia went on an emotional roller coaster ride. She started with worry. Worried that maybe something had happened to him. Then she moved on to anger. Angry that yet again, he had disappointed her. Then she became hurt and sad. She went to her room where she called him enough times to fill up his voicemail box. She figured once she filled up the voicemail, she could keep calling to see if it stayed full. She was embarrassed to think she was reduced to these antics. She changed clothes and decided to go to his house. When she got there, she knocked on the door, no answer. Julia called Kevin's phone and got voice mail again. She angered more when she figured out that his voice mail had been emptied. She left him a new message. Julia went from having a fabulous day to this. She couldn't believe she actually popped up at his house. How did she come to this? Is Kevin poison? He lied time and time again and she knew it. She had grown to accept his inconsistent behavior.

She didn't know how to get out of this relationship though. He made her feel so good most of the time. Lately, he was inconsistent. When they were apart, she always ended up regretting having met him. When they were together, she never wanted it to end. She knew she would lose her mind if she continued this journey with him. She had to end this. She went home.

Julia laid in bed thinking about Kevin. She thought of the money he had borrowed and how cloudy her memory was as to whether he paid it back or not. She seemed to be giving more than she was getting back even though he did a lot for her. She hoped he would never call her again. Then her phone rang. It was Kevin.

Next Day He'd Keep It Cool

Julia looked at the clock, it was 3 am. She couldn't believe he had the audacity to call her at 3 am after basically standing her up. This was a pattern that she was not going to let him start.

"Yes Kevin"
"Hey baby, how are you?"
"What do you want Kevin?"
"Damn baby, you awake?"
"What do you want Kevin!"
"Can I come over?"
"Why?"
"I need to see you"
"Why? What do you want?"
"Please baby, I need you."

Julia's heart melted at his words. Why did he have this effect on her? Why did she long for him? She wanted to say yes. Her senses were over powered by his charm. He had her.

"What happened to you earlier?"
"That's why I need to see you. I need to talk."
"Something happened, that's why I wasn't there. Something happened to my ex, Janae. Please can I come over? Don't be mad at me please. Say yes."
"Ok, come on." Julia was so weak for him.

Julia was anxious and wanted to see him. Maybe she needed to see him.

"I love you Julia."

She hung up the phone. Julia was surprised by his profession of love for her. He had never said it and for some reason she needed to hear it. She got up and brushed her teeth and her hair. She desperately wanted to know what had happened and why it caused him to no-show her party.

Kevin walked into her bedroom where she had fallen asleep in a chair while waiting for him. She was tired and disoriented. How did he get in? Oh yeah, her spare key. She wished he'd give it back but she didn't have the heart to ask for it and have him think she didn't trust him.

Kevin leaned in to kiss her and she turned up her cheek. She was fuming mad, again. He apologized that it took so long to get there but that he was at the hospital. The story gets interesting from here.

"Hey baby, sorry I am late. I was at Memorial Hospital with Janae's family."

"Hospital? *(Sitting up straight and intently staring at him for his next words)* What happened?"

"She called me earlier, told me she wanted to reconcile. I refused her advances and she threatened to kill herself. She said she had a gun and was going to shoot herself if I didn't come to her. She said she'd do it right on the phone. She let me listen as she cocked the gun. I called her parents and headed over there. I kept her on the phone the entire time as I was in transit. She sounded serious."

"Why didn't you tell me this, call me earlier to let me know?"

"I'm sorry; I was preoccupied and just didn't think. I'm sorry baby. I would die if I lost you! Don't be mad please. I didn't know what to do!"

"I don't understand. *(Not buying it entirely)* How'd you end up at the hospital?"

"When I got there, she looked weird. I saw an empty bottle on the table. She took some pills, all of a bottle and she passed out when I got there. I called 911 and went to the hospital in the ambulance with her. I was scared."

Kevin cried real tears and this melted Julia's hardened heart. She reached over and hugged him closely. She was sad but full of questions. She didn't know how any of this would affect her life, but, Kevin was in pain and she aimed to comfort him. She held him close until he kissed her neck softly. He moved from her neck, to her chest, then her breast through her silk nighty. He lifted her shirt and caressed her nipple. He whispered how much he loved her and was glad he had her.

He told her how much he needed her. His hands were all over, plotting, sculpting over her every curve. He lifted her up and placed her on her bed. He pushed her low on the pillows and pulled down her satin sleep shorts. He placed his mouth firmly over her secret and caressed her in a french-kiss-like-way until she abruptly came into his mouth. He came up to lay next to her. She wanted more but he motioned her to lay on his chest. He didn't want to do anything more than cuddle. That was sweet to Julia. She consented to just a cuddle. Julia reciprocated warmly and was glad he was there. She then forgot to be upset with him. Julia said a prayer for Kevin's ex-wife Janae.

As time passed, they laid there, she wondered why he had had time to clear his voicemail but not time to call her back. She allowed the mood to cover her curiosity. Still, she thought she would like to meet Janae and if things were different, she could even help Janae through what she was going through. Julia had no idea what would happen next with this Janae-Kevin situation.

Her alarm went off at 6:30 a.m. as usual. When she reached to silence it, she immediately noticed, Kevin was gone.

Thinking I'm His Fool

"Hey baby!" Kevin spoke in a low whisper.

"Why the hell did you leave without telling me!" More of an accusation than a question.

"Damn Julia! Can I at least get a hi or hello or something?"

"Don't bull shit me! Dammit Kevin! Why'd you leave?"

"Where are you?"

"Look dammit! *(Still a low whisper)* I'm at the hospital, not that I have to answer to you Julia, or anyone else for that matter! Watch how you talk to me while you're at it!"

"Ok. *(Calmly)* Sorry, but you look, that was very rude to leave without saying bye. That's not fair Kevin."

"I didn't want to wake you! I felt you needed your rest after such a long day, the party, and me coming over so late! I was doing you a favor." He was very annoyed with her she could tell.

"Why are you there so early? It's barely 7 am. Why are you there? Where's her damn family!"

"Damn Jules, why are you sweating me so hard! I don't owe you an explanation for everything I do! I ain't one of those sorry losers you're used to pushing around and handling any kind of way girl! You might want to check to see who's in charge here! Calm the f' down. I got a call she was awake, so I wanted to check on her. FYI, I can do what I damn well please!"

Kevin hung up the phone on her. Julia sat there for a moment then tried calling him back. She knew damn well he didn't have the audacity to hang up. Maybe she was being rude and even bossy towards him. But why did he handle her so roughly! She thought. If they are over, why is he acting like she's so important? She has her family! Ugh! Kevin didn't answer any of Julia's calls. She called several times. No answer though. Finally, hours later he called her back.

"Hey Jules."

"Hey Kevin."

"Look I am sorry about earlier and about not taking your calls. I'm just really worried and I feel guilty, like all of her problems are my fault. I know you don't understand this, but, I need you to back off on the jealous girlfriend role and trust me."

"Jealous girlfriend? Is that how I'm acting?"

Maybe she was acting like a jealous girlfriend. She played dumb though, but agreed to stop with all of the questions, if they were unnecessary ones.

"Yes Julia, you sounded like I was cheating on you or something. I love you and want to be with only you. That's it."

"Ok, I get it. I wasn't jealous, just annoyed. You've been very inconsistent. I feel like you have a disregard for my feelings. I'm sorry, I didn't mean for us to fight Kevin. How is she?"

"Who?"

"Janae!" Julia snapped, suddenly very pissed off again.

"She is better; she's going to be fine."

"Oh, you spoke to the doctors?"

"Yes, she'll be fine."

"Great. So, are you in her room, still at the hospital?"

"No. I am home. Just got here."

"Oh, that's good."

Julia was worried about this situation. Kevin sounded like he wasn't saying something. She felt like he was not being honest, but, she had no idea about what. She decided to end the call and enjoy some me-time of her own. Kevin had different plans.

"Kevin, go ahead and relax for a while, I will talk with you later."

"No, I need you. Come and go to my mom's house with me. She's having us all over for early dinner at her house later. You can meet her; she's been dying to meet you. That way we can hang out for a while."

Julia agreed. She needed to see him as well. Plus, she could ask him more questions about Janae and find out how she's doing now. She wanted to put her uneasiness to rest.

About halfway through the day, she found herself staring blindly into her closet. Julia wanted to make a good impression on Kevin's mom. She knew she would anyway, but, still she wanted to look extra special. She worried that her lack of rest would show heavily on her face. As she looked in her mirror, she gently caressed her face and rubbed her eyes. She looked and felt tired. Julia decided to take a short nap first. She called Kevin back to make sure what time he wanted to meet. She told him she wanted a short nap. He gave her directions to his mom's house and told her to come around 4 or 5. They agreed to meet there and Julia relaxed on her chaise lounge for a good nap.

Wife Was His Goal

"Kevin, I'm turning on your mom's street now."

"Ok baby, I will come outside. Come to the cul-de-sac, she's on the right. You'll see my car. I'll be standing in her driveway."

"Oh ok, I see you now."

"Yeah, park right here." Kevin pointed to where he wanted her to park.

He motioned her to an open spot in the small cul-de-sac. His mom lived in an older community, well kept, in East Houston. Her yard was detailed and well-manicured with beautiful seasonal flowers and lush green grass. Julia saw great curb appeal and a quaint elevation. She felt Mrs. Jones must have been there for a while by the looks of her overstuffed garage.

She parked and got out of her car as Kevin swiftly embraced her and swept her off of her feet. He kissed her with longing passion, she knew where that kiss would lead.

She was happy to see him and decided not to mention Janae unless he did first. Maybe they both needed to just have fun. He asked her how she was doing and if she enjoyed her nap. She told him it was the best rest she'd had in days and she needed the rest.

They went inside and Kevin introduced Julia to his mom, sister, two brothers and a nephew. There were also a few neighbors visiting. They were all nice. His mom was about 5 feet tall and maybe 140 pounds. She was well endowed in the chest and small from the waist down. Her hair was simple but cared for. She had a mom hair style, like of those roller-sets older ladies get. She wore a peculiar fragrance that reminded Julia of roses, which she hates. She truly couldn't stand the smell of red roses.

Kevin's moms' house was neat and modestly furnished, but to Julia's dismay, the sofa was covered in plastic. Julia wondered if folks still did such an ancient thing as covering furniture in plastic. Now she knew they did. She smiled inside. Even with the plastic covered furniture, the house was very warm and inviting. Kevin went to take a call while his mom entertained Julia. She was nice and very talkative.

She told Julia stories about the type of child Kevin was. She told Julia story after story. She began to talk about Janae and told Julia that she would be happiest when Kevin gets totally away from Janae. She said Janae was lazy and manipulative. She spoke so much about Janae *(while never mentioning the suicide attempt)* that Julia had the strange feeling that she knew nothing about the suicide attempt. Just as she was about to ask Mrs. Jones about the suicide, Kevin returned to the room. She decided to wait. He had shown Julia his temper a couple of times and she didn't want to upset him in front of his family.

"Hey ladies! What's going on? What are we talking about? Julia, don't let my mom tell you those wild stories about me when I was a kid. Half of it ain't true and the other half is false." Kevin had the prettiest teeth. His smile lit up the room.

At that moment Kevin's sister Tonia chimed in...

"Oh yes! It's definitely all true! *(As she kissed her brother on the cheek)* How'd you meet this loser anyways Julia? You seem a bit out of his league." Tonia winked Julia and smiled slyly at her own words.

"Well, *(she kissed his other cheek)* and all this time, I thought he was out of my league!"

They all laughed.

"Hahaha! Well, we met in the line of work. Julia is a real estate broker. She's Mr. Fontana's agent. A very good one too! She begged me to go out with her, and, you know I have a soft spot for beautiful women!" He winked and reciprocated their kisses on the cheek.

Julia's eyes widened. She laughed her infectious laugh. Kevin's mom was smitten with Julia. She stared at her with the warmest eyes. Julia was easy to fall in love with. She was genuine and personable.

His mom had set a very nice table. Tonia handed Julia a flute of champagne. They toasted to Kevin and his love for beautiful women. Everyone congregated around the lavishly decorated table. She had gone all out with 4th of July décor. Julia loved holidays so this was extremely appealing to her. As they sipped champagne and enjoyed their meal, Julia noticed the attention Kevin received from his own family. They worshipped him. This was an unusual amount of love. This love was not distributed among Mrs. Jones other kids but, was spilled all over Kevin. He was their star player and he could do no wrong in their eyes. Oddly, no one mentioned Janae at all. If this was Julia's family, they wouldn't have made it through their greetings without mentioning someone's ex.

His mom was a good hostess. She cleared the dishes and refused help. Julia insisted and washed dishes too. Mrs. Jones smiled gently and loved every minute she spent with Julia in her kitchen. Tonia gladly retired into a small TV room with Kevin and her brothers. As they cleaned the kitchen, Julia asked Mrs. Jones if she knew how Janae was. The mom seemed surprised but told Julia she assumed Janae was fine. Then Mrs. Jones changed the subject fast. Julia pressed the issue and went back to the subject of Janae.

"So, when will Janae be released?"
"Released?" Mrs. Jones seemed unaware of Janae's situation.
"Yes, from the hospital? You know right?"

"Umm. Yes, I know. Kevin has all of the details sweetheart. Let's ask him now." *She moved as if to leave the kitchen but Julia grabbed her arm gently.*

"No. *(Smiling softly)* It can wait. Let him enjoy his siblings."

She smiled wearily as she concluded Kevin's mom obviously knew nothing about Janae's attempted suicide.

"Mrs. Jones, I love your kitchen. Who redid your kitchen? I see signs of a remodel."

They talked for a while and set the table for desert. Julia had a small piece of the best sweet potato pie she had ever had in her entire life. His mom wasn't the best cook but, the food was decent. She could bake a mean pie though! Julia wanted more but, refrained. Kevin grabbed her hand and took her to his old room. It was still decorated like a little boys room. He even had current effects in there. Kevin said he spends a lot of time there helping his mom so he keeps clothes and stuff there just in case he spent the night.

It was getting a little late for Julia so she said her goodbyes. Kevin's mom hugged Julia and made her promise to come again. She even told Kevin that Julia would make a fine daughter-n-law. Those words made Julia smile.

"That's my goal momma, that's my goal." Kevin smiled a boyish smile looking dead smack at Julia.

She Called On My Phone

Julia was saying her goodbyes to Kevin's family; it had been a long enough visit. She had a very nice time at his mom's house and thanked Ms. Jones for everything and for having her over. It was nice. Julia was very much at ease and looked forward to many days like this in the future.

She put her seat belt on and put her car in gear. While backing out of the driveway, her cell phone rang. It was an unfamiliar number and briefly she wondered who it could be. She pulled off down the street. She ignored the unknown caller. The phone rang again. She ignored it. It rang again, so she finally answered. It was a call no woman wanted to receive.

"Hello."
"Hi Julia?"
"Umm who's this?"
"Janae Jones, Kevin's wife."

Julia's heart fell to the floor of her car. What the heck! But, maybe she heard incorrectly.

"Janae? *(Gasping for air)* Don't you mean ex-wife?"
"No sweetie, I said what I meant, wife. I'm still his wife. Do you have a minute?"
"NO! I do not. I'm sure you need to call him, not me."

She hung up the phone. *What the heck is she calling me for? How'd she get my cell phone number anyway? Is she out of the hospital?* Ring. Her cell phone rang again.

"I know she's not calling me again!" Phone rang again.

"Hello!" In a very sharp annoyed tone, Julia answered again.

"Please Julia, don't hang up. This won't take long. Please hear me out." Janae's voice was hurried and desperate.

"Look why are you calling me? Are you out of the hospital?"

"Hospital? Where'd you get that from? *(Janae dismissed the hospital remark)* He's still my husband and I'm calling you to get you to leave him alone. *(Her words were stalled and didn't sound very truthful)* We have 4 kids two are his. He lives with us but probably appears to live with his mom or elsewhere while me and these kids are constantly without food, vehicle, etc. I want you to leave him alone so we can fix our marriage." Janae seemed to be unsure of her request. Silence fell over the line.

"Yeah, he told me about you. I didn't figure you'd call me, but, ok thanks for the info. *(Trying to conceal her anxiety as she reached to end the call)* Glad to hear you recovered from your suicide attempt." Taking a jab at her in retaliation.

"Suicide? Let me guess. He said I tried to kill myself?"

"I have to go bye!"

"Wait, I know stuff, things you would not want me to know."

"I don't think so."

"I know you gave him $500 the other morning. It was four $100 bills and five $20 bills which you spilled coffee on."

"What? *(Speechless)* H-hhow do you know that?" Pain overcame Julia as Janae went on.

"Because he gave most of it to me. Like I said, I'm his wife. He always brings it home to me. Check your email, I sent you copies of the court records and marriage license. I knew you wouldn't believe me."

"Really, maybe it's fake." Julia smarted back at her defensively.

"Maybe it isn't. You love him?" Janae questioned.

"What?" How much do I give to this conversation, Julia thought.

"I know you love him. That's what he wants and he's good at getting it. He's the fake, he has this whole plan to get money out of you. We are BOTH taking you for a ride. It's a con!"

We are, we are, we are. All Julia could hear are those two words. "We are" as they replayed over and over in her head.

"What! What the hell are you talking about Janae? He wouldn't—"

"We" would. Listen, just check your email. Whatever you do, don't tell him I called. He will just lie and we will both lose. That deal you're working on with him, the big one, it's far bigger than you think. Call him and say exactly what I tell you."

Janae Jones had Julia's full attention. Her mind raced as she listened to Janae's words. Janae told her what to say to Kevin and they both hung up.

Janae Jones sat lowly on her sofa. She was shaking with nerves. Had she done the right thing? She had spent the last month studying Julia. Watching her, reading her emails and texts to her husband. That bitch! Janae wanted to hate her. Truth is, if Julia was a guy she'd be in love with her too! This lady was nice. Janae watched from her car as Julia came and went from her office. She watched her and Kevin out on dates. She had surveyed every part of Julia's life. She even interviewed with Julia for a new agent sponsorship job in a wig and heavy makeup. She was already feeling bad for Julia but back then her love for Kevin ruled her entire being.

Janae knew deep inside she had to expose Kevin. She'd come to the conclusion that Julia was too innocent person to continue with their scam but could both benefit if Julia would play along. Julia was a harmless lady. The kind of person you'd want as a friend. She had done her homework on Julia and couldn't find a single reason not to like her, except of course, if her husband was falling for her. Now that she knew he hadn't put Julia first, before her, she almost felt sorry for Julia. Sorry for what "they" had planned for her.

Janae had been there with Kevin for 10 years, thick and thin through all of his bullshit and all of Kevin's schemes and plots. They had made a living off of conning people. It was just that simple. He'd consumed her and she allowed it as long as she got to keep him. Julia was the last of her worries. Kevin knew he could never keep a straight laced girl like Julia. So it was definitely all an act. He was out of his league. He and Janae were taking Julia for a ride she would have soon regretted had Janae not made the call. But, Janae didn't do it for Julia. She was on board with Kevin sleeping with Julia and all that comes with that con. What upset Janae was that she stumbled across Kevin's other "other woman".

This one was unauthorized! Plus the other "other" woman was pregnant to boot! She began spying on him when she noticed hours in his day went by that were unaccounted for and he was not with Julia, as she thought. She followed him and saw for herself as he scooped his little pregnant chick up and took her to doctor's appointments. That's when she had to think quickly and come up with a plan. Her plan was to bring him down, all the way down at that and be done with him forever. She knew Julia wouldn't listen to her at first. She needed to find the right words that would make Julia hear her out. She had decided to start with the unhappy wife wanting her hubby back. When that didn't move Julia, she went out on a limb and came clean *(clean for Janae Jones anyway)*.

Janae was hurting beyond all understanding. She thought he loved her. Silly of her to think she was a priority in his life. He actually cheated on her! No con, no hustle. Did he love this new chick? Was it his baby? Of course it was, she found the ultrasound behind the ashtray in his car. She had no friends, he made sure of that. She was totally alone. Even her family didn't like how she lived and the things they assumed he did. She had no one to turn to. She had their four children and no one to turn to except Julia.

In her twisted mind and savage love for him, she could tolerate anything Kevin did as long as he was faithful. How would their plans for the future be affected by his "girlfriend and baby momma"? She cried and cried and cried. She didn't understand what his next move would be but she wasn't going to help him bring Julia down and get all the money just so he could run off and be with some other chick! That was for sure. He had told her they really needed to get the divorce so he could marry Julia then get the money and divorce Julia and remarry her. Maybe that was not the plan at all. Maybe it was the pregnant baby momma he would marry.

It was time. She was tired of all of the lying they did to escape actually working for their living. That life was growing old on her. She was never happy, never at peace. It was time to get out, forever. She was so fed up with all of the scheming and lying they did. It was time for her to get away from him for good.

Julia sat in her car numb. She didn't realize she had been in this vacant parking lot for tens of minutes. Her heart was beating fast, body trembling, tears flowing. Could this be true? How'd she know about the $500 she had reluctantly given to Kevin? Julia replayed in her mind all the times she had given him money. Lately, he was lazy about giving it back too. What was going on? Was she being played? What should she do now? She pulled up the email on her blackberry. Of course the image wasn't the best quality, but she could clearly tell he was still married. She replayed the last thirty days in her head. Dating him, the countless hours spent talking; the many hours spent walking, the dancing, etc.

Her cell rang and interrupted her thoughts. It was Kevin.

"Hey baby! You made it home safe?"

"No, I'm just sitting at my desk grabbing a file I needed." She lied, she was in a random parking lot between his mom's house and her own home.

"Hmmm, what file?"

"Just a file. Janae just called me Kevin."

"What! *(Loudly)* What did that lying bitch want! Don't believe a word!"

He mouthed word for word what Janae said he would say.

"She said you're still married and she wants me to leave you alone. Said she knows you love me and wishes I would walk away from you so you'd give your marriage another chance. Be honest, are you still married?"

"Is that all she said?"

"Yes, is it true?"

"Julia, be honest, are you sure that's everything she said?" Kevin was trying to stay calm but he was yelling mad.

"Yes! Damn it! That's all she said. Are you still married to her?" Julia yelled back at him.

"It's not like that. She just won't sign the papers! Legally yes, but in my heart, no!"

"You lied to me! You damn liar! What else? What else did you lie about?" Her mind stopped spinning when he said legally "yes". He didn't say no! How could he admit it? He lied this long now he's not denying it?

"Wait a minute! Slow down, there's no more lies! I promise, that's all that's it! I swear."

"You have kids?"

"She said that? She's lying! They're her kids, not mines."

"No she didn't say that. *(Julia lied again)* Since you're a liar, I figured that was just another one of your lies. You didn't tell me she had kids. You said yall didn't have kids. She didn't mention kids just that she wants her husband back."

"Julia that's not fair. WE didn't, don't have children. Come on, never mind, I'm on my way to you."

"NO! I'm going home. Do not dare come to me! I need to process this. We can talk tomorrow." She knew he'd press the issue.

"Hell no! I'm meeting you there!" Kevin hung up on her. Just as Janae said. He was coming to her.

Julia started her car engine. Laid her head on her steering wheel consumed with shock. She picked her head up once again and embraced what seemed like a long drive home. She wondered what she had gotten herself into this time.

About 20 minutes later she was home. She was just getting out of a hot shower when she heard Kevin's voice calling out for her. It was startling; she hadn't gotten that damn spare key back from him. Now that she thought back to when she loaned it to him, maybe that was a part of the scheme. He wanted the key. Janae had told her so much, too much. She had exposed Kevin's lies. Julia suddenly realized, she had been a part of a huge lie. She was living a lie. Everything that had happened between her and this man, who she loved, was a lie. He lied to her a thousand times.

"I'm in here Kevin" She gasped solemnly.

He walked over to her, he put his arms around her wet body draped in her towel, and pulled her close to him into a warm hug. Julia felt nausea overcome her. Love can turn to hate so fast.

"Oh God. That crazy bitch! I can't lose you! Not so soon, not now. I'm so sorry. I just thought it'd be done by now. So sorry she upset you with those awful lies baby. You ok? I've been ringing your doorbell for a while. I still have the key so I let myself in."

"You bastard!" That lie threw her over the edge, she forgot to pretend. She began beating him off of her.

She broke away from his hold, hitting him and slapping him in the chest and face. Unable to completely do what Janae had urged her to do. Her real emotions came out. She was in love with him. She fell hard for him and this is what a woman does when she is scorned by her man.

"You fucking liar! How could you lie to me!"

Kevin grabbed her by her wrists, stopping her from hitting him further. His grip sobered her. She moved her emotions back to the plan Janae laid out for her.

"I know! I know everything! You are married! I can't believe you lied!"

"Wait, wait wait! *(Julia tried to free herself of his hold)* It is over, but, she keeps refusing to sign the papers. I thought it would be over long before now! Listen to me! Don't let this crazy bitch ruin us. I don't want to lose you! I'm serious. As soon as this deal closes the divorce will be final. She only wants money. She doesn't want me back, she lied to you. I'm so close; please forgive me for lying or omitting."

He pulled her back to his chest, tilting her head up to him as she gave in and stopped fighting it. He looked genuine, even as he lied. What a sweet beautiful liar he was. Nothing he had ever said was the truth to Julia, now that he had lied.

"Please forgive me?" Kevin was a damn good looking man. He lied so well. He knelt to her, almost as if he'd propose right there. His eyes were beautiful and full of sorrow. Maybe he has reasons. She wanted to believe him but her gut told her not to.

"Ok, so you filed, she won't sign. You don't live with her and her kids? The kids are not yours? This is the total truth?"

"Yes, that's what I've been trying to say, the whole truth baby I promise. She is lying. She wants you to run. Please don't run."

"I just can't believe this!" Julia was both acting out what Janae said in order to get to the truth, as well as, reacting fully as a woman would in such a situation. She paced the floor trying to get back to the plan, leery of who to trust or what to do next.

"Come on baby, we're having such a good time. Say you'll forgive this. You ok?" He pulled her close again.

"Ok. Yes, I'm ok, just tired. I'm going to bed. You staying?"

Parts of her hoped he'd stay and make a liar out of his wife. But as they hugged tightly, Julia frowned because she surely didn't want him touching her now if he was leaving.

"Uh no, I've got to help momma get shut down and my brother can't stay with her tonight so I already promised I'd stay with her tonight. But come here." His heart was so cold but his hands were warm, maybe even hot. Julia still hoped there was a shadow of a doubt that he was not lying. She'd know soon.

Kevin pulled her close again after noticing she'd pulled away again and began kissing her from her cheeks down to her belly button. She wanted to resist but let go as she momentarily forgot the anger and hurt she had felt minutes ago. Julia was more than confused. He was confusing. Almost convincing. Maybe Janae was lying. Maybe he was trying to get away from her. Maybe this is just some crazy ex drama. For a moment she believed her maybes. She allowed him to drop her towel from her naked body and relaxed as he tasted the sweet taste of her sex. She came quickly and he kissed her belly button slowly making circles on it with his delicious tongue. He has talent for sure, sexual talent. He ended sweetly and went to her bathroom.

She could hear him brushing his teeth and the sound of the running water as he probably cleansed his face. She quickly grabbed her black satin bathrobe. He returned with a sexy smile and said he was off. At that moment Julia felt a world of contempt for him. She had to be one of the dumbest females she knew at that point. Everything made sense now. Janae's last words to her rang so true right then. *"He will come to your house to lie some more, convince you I'm crazy. Then he will come to me and spend the night, trying to lie to me more and sexing me all night long. He will not sleep with you because he will save it for me. We get quite a work out and there is usually nothing left for anyone else. Maybe he will try to please you orally, I don't know. But, he will need to do something sexual to get you off his scent. So, watch. I know him. That is his signature. You'll see Julia. You'll see."*

She forced herself to return his kiss and barely kissed his lips as he kissed her. She wanted to vomit. Her mind was racing, replaying everything. Trying to wrap her mind around what had happened, what was happening, what was going to happen from here.

"We good?" His strong hands on her cheeks smelled of Dove soap and her PE360 lotion. Idiot.

"I'm fine Kevin, *(she knew he didn't totally believe her)* and yes we are good. Call me and let me know you made it ok?"

"Of course." He tilted her head and kisses her softly.

He left, she saw to it he was gone and made sure he drove off. After about 15 minutes, just as she expected, Janae called on her phone, again.

"I know he's gone he just called me and is on his way to me. He is pissed at me for calling you Julia."

"Really?" Julia wasn't very surprised.

"I'll call you when he gets here. I won't say a word; I'll just let you listen. Be sure to mute your phone. We cannot get caught. I want to let you hear first-hand, his lies. That way you and me can move forward with the plan."

"Uhh, ok. He said exactly what you said he would say."

"How was it? Did you let him uhh?"

"Yes, he went down on me if that's what you're asking. I let him. You were right." Julia was saddened to hear her own words. Her admission to her boyfriend's wife spoke volumes to where she was in life at this moment.

"Yeah, he's very persuasive. I'm not mad, you can tell me details if you want. I'm used to it. He lets me listen to yall sometimes."

"Unbelievable! I've got to go! This makes me sick to my stomach! FYI, I don't want to know you! We are not friends. I needed to know what you've told me. But make no mistake, we are not friends! Just call me like you said you would when he gets there!" The click of the phone seemed so loud it echoed loudly over her room.

Julia put her phone down. She reached over for her bible and put Lee Williams's cd in and it played "I Can't Give Up". This song always gave Julia the strength that only God could give. This time it felt as if it would break her to the core. She refused to break, she wiped a lone year away and stifled the ones that threatened to follow.

She was reading from Psalms when tears raced down her face. She wiped and wiped but they kept coming. Determined not to fall apart, she placed her hand on her chest. Her heart beat so loud and so fast she felt she was having some kind of attack. Maybe it's a heart attack? She breathed in the air so fast she couldn't catch her breath. She moaned softly as she tried to gain control, "No no no!" rung from her lips as they trembled in sorrow. She had lost the just-hold-it-together battle.

She had been holding on to so much anger and so many fears, and so much of everything. Hiding her problems from the world, being so alone from the world. She knew tears would not help and took another deep breath and moved on. No tears for Julia, this time.

Lies So Deep They Cut Just Like a Knife

It took Julia the entire day to pull herself out of bed. When she woke up it was almost noon. She had missed church, which she needed more than ever in her life. She rushed to get dressed and make at least half of the twelve o'clock service. Service was good. She made it just in time to see Pastor West preach. His words were directed towards her. How'd he know what she was going through? God has a way of doing that, making a service just what you need. She was very happy she went and was ready for whatever came her way now, so she thought. When she got back to her car, bible in hand, she sat in her seat and said a little prayer. She started the engine and decided to check her messages and missed calls before she drove off. She had missed several calls from Janae and not one from Kevin. Why hadn't he called? What had happened?

Last thing Julia remembered, was when Janae called last night and let her listen to their conversation once Kevin arrived to "their" house. He was very angry calling her all kinds of bitches and whores and more. Why'd Janae let him do her like that? Listening to that was so exhausting. She remembered him giving Janae all sorts of promises and bullshit.

"Janae, you know I only have a heart for you. I mess with these bitches because we need me to. This is for you baby, for us. We need this so we can start a new life. We won't be in old man Fontana's path anymore. He won't be able to dangle all his wealth in my face anymore. You know what that feels like to be spoon fed! A grown ass man like me being reduced to being a flunky! Driving his cars, living in his house! Damn near cleaning up his shit every time he shits! I thought you were down with me. Come here girl."

Julia could hear kissing and moans. The conversation went like this.

"So she doesn't mean anything to you then?" Janae begged.

"Hell no! Stuck up bougee ass bitch can't compare to you babe! Come on now, you know how we do. Come here let me hit that ass for you."

"Why haven't I talked to you much for the last two days then?"

Janae kept him at arm's length with her hand extended out to his chest, aware of Julia listening. She wanted to put on a good show for Julia, needing to convince Julia and convince her well.

"Because I've been stroking Julia. Damn I came by and brought the money to you. Did you get groceries? Feed the kids?"

"Yes. Thanks. Still I don't like not hearing from you! Don't do that again!"

"I'm sorry babe, but I can't be calling you every five minutes and still convince Julia I want to be with her and marry her. Shit don't match. Cut me some slack. You used to be so cool with this. What changed?"

"She's beautiful. Yall have a strong chemistry."

"Heck no! She's cool; outside of you a bitch is a bitch! But she'd turn her snooty nose at me if she knew what I was really about. She'd never be with a guy like me, the real me. Bitches like that want a corporate dude with all kinds of money. She wants a nigga to take her around the world. Fucked up chicks like that, always wanting more, needing to go somewhere else. She's a lot of fucking work! I'm so tired of this shit with her ass anyway. Babe I love you and I only want you, no one else. You and this money we bout to get from Julia's ass. It's about the hustle baby. You know that, right? Stick to the plan! Damn! Think 9 million dollars. It's not going to be that much longer."

"The sex?" She knew he was lying, but she hoped he wasn't.

"It's a job, work, come here baby, let me get in that ass. You're all I want. Come on! You jealous? It was work. Julia is work. A lot of work."

"NO! I want to know if you enjoy the sex." Janae pushed him further. As far as she could. At this point she was hoping to hurt Julia, even though she knew she shouldn't keep pushing him.

Julia had to hang up at this point. She couldn't bare anymore. She went to her bar and had a drink, then another drink. She just needed to pass out and not feel a thing. She wanted to be numb.

As Julia checked her call logs, Janae called her several times and she finally answered. Even as she held the phone, Janae was blowing her up.

"What?"

"You heard when I called last night?" Julia could hear her smiling through the phone.

"Yes, most of it."

"Most? Why'd you hang up?"

"Unlike you Janae, I couldn't stand to listen to my man fuck another woman, not even his wife."

"Oh, I'm sorry. I forgot you're "that" girl. Must be nice. Well, meet me anyway just like we planned, we got work to do."

"No, thank you. I'm all set."

"Well you might want to know he left here and is now with his baby momma. If you change your mind about meeting me, I will be at TGIF on 290 at 2:30 and I will stay until 3 o'clock pm. If you show up, we will do business. If you don't, I will leave by 3. FYI, I'm doing this with or without you so I suggest you man up and stop this fucker from fucking you, next time it won't be consensual." Without waiting for a reply Janae hung up.

As Julia sat in the church parking lot, she shook off the urge to replay Janae's and Kevin's conversation. She looked at the clock and decided to go to meet with Janae Jones.

Julia entered the restaurant and sat at the bar. It was 2:30pm on the dot. Janae said she'd be wearing all white.

"Hello Julia." Janae stood behind Julia.

Julia turned around and was taken off guard by this stark beauty. This woman was Hollywood beautiful. She caught herself from dropping her mouth to the floor. Why in the hell did she put up with the life Kevin had provided for her! Janae had on tight white jeans with crystal stone embellishments on the side stitching. Her blouse was low cut and she smelled of one of those Victoria Secret cheap scents. Her hair was fine, long and naturally curly, and pulled back behind her ears. She wore diamond studs and a huge gaudy wedding ring on her left hand ring finger. Ouch! That hurt Julia a little.

"You're Janae?"
"Yes! But, wow, you're prettier than I thought" She already knew that, but pretended to meet Julia for the first time.

"As are you." Julia still couldn't figure out why someone who looked like Janae stayed with a loser like Kevin.

"I'm sorry Julia."

She extended her hand to shake Julia's but Julia didn't receive it. Janae withdrew her hand and took a seat.

"I know you're hurting Julia, but, thanks for trusting me. You had no reason to."

"I don't trust you; I felt I had little choice. But, thank you. I would have never known if you hadn't called. So, we've got that out of the way, what happens now in your plan? Where's the stuff?"

"Here it is" She handed Julia a bag.

"I'm listening." Julia looked into the bag.

Janae broke down her plan and even though she was shocked and overwhelmed, Julia agreed to play along and give it a try. At this point, she only had one thing on her mind, and that was getting this deal closed and leaving Kevin the hell alone.

"Don't open the bag here, let's go somewhere else. Come and ride with me, that way we can talk and ride."

"Why should I do that? I can look at it here."

"Look *(fury and impatience in her eyes)* this ain't no fucking! We're not in a damn fairy tale movie! Grow the fuck up! We don't have much time. When I don't call him by a certain time or answer his call, he will wonder what's up. Now come on!"

Julia looked hesitant. How did she end up here, with her boyfriend's wife, plotting his demise? She should have walked away, but, that seemed to be a choice she didn't have. She was lost but very curious about how deep Kevin's lies ran.

"Do you want to know or not? I'm doing this with or without your ass just like I said earlier. Get out of your damn feelings! Let's go."

Janae stood up and walked towards the door. Julia followed her. Somehow, Janae walked straight towards Julia's car. Of course, she's been studying Julia for months. Janae smiled and said.

"Nice car! Love it."
"Thanks." Julia's tone was sour.
"Here I am the white truck. It's my dad's."

Janae opened the door of the old worn out white truck and Julia followed. She looked at how dirty and full of kids' toys, food, clothing and debris it was. She was afraid to touch anything. How could a woman so beautiful live like this. She was actually afraid.

They went to a nearby hotel around the corner. Janae said she rented the room for privacy, told Julia the videos she had were graphic. Julia was nervous, very nervous. The wife showed her videos on a portable DVD player, pictures, bank records, etc. and mapped out everything they had planned for Julia. Janae showed Julia every email, text, phone call, etc. that she and Kevin had sent back and forth. Many of the emails were personal and racy. She let Julia listen to the recordings of several sexual escapades and telephone conversations between Julia and Kevin. She could even hear the con artist and wife laughing. It was very bad and very crast.

"You ok? Had enough yet?"

"Yeah, turn it off." Julia was packing everything up.

"Now, are you ready for the one lie I have told you?"

"Oh shit! What li--" As Julia was about to ask what lie, the door knocked. Someone was at the door.

"That's my one lie."

Couldn't Last For Long

"Lie? Who the hell could that be?" Julia stood up and grabbed her purse and the bag of "lies".

"Oh well, uh, uh, uh that's"

"What the fu--" Janae covered her mouth.

"Shhhhh! Be quiet. Now, I didn't tell you because I wanted you to see the proof first. Now, that's him. Follow my lead. I warned you we didn't have much time. Our plan begins now."

"Why the hell is he here! (In an angered whisper). Why the fuck is he here! I'm out! You crazy dysfunctional bitch!" Janae covered her mouth again.

Julia bit her hand and moved towards the door. She was in deeper than she wanted to be and now was the perfect time to get out, she thought.

"Ouch! Damn you! Ouch! You really want to fuck this all up? You're in deep bitch! You'd better get your fucking head in the game and quick! He'll take the deal away! You'll get nothing! Then what was all this for? Think! You'll lose everything!"

"Alright! Alright! If you lie to me one more time it's over. Don't trick me!"

"Go into the bathroom, get undressed down to your bra and panties, if I remember correctly you always match and it looks like sexy lingerie. Is that true today?"

"Why? *(Confused about where this is going)*. Yes, true."

"Just curious. Come out in 10 minutes. Time it correctly. Just 10 minutes after he's in here. Play along like we're having a three way, for his birthday. You can do this!" Janae noticed Julia's horrified facial expression.

"His birthday? *(She didn't know it was his birthday)* I'm not into that sort of thing. I...don't do three-somes!"

"Think $9 million dollars and see what you come up with. We won't actually have to do anything. Hmm, *(she paused and looked Julia up and down as if she was asking a question with no words leaving her mouth)* of course you didn't know it was his birthday. Come on, you can do this."

Julia went into the bathroom. Janae pulled out wine glasses and strawberries. She removed her jeans quickly as she waited for Kevin's call. She knew he'd go back to his car to use his phone which he strategically left in the car to prevent getting caught communicating with the baby momma. He was so predictable. She was ready by the time the phone rang.

Julia went to the bathroom and did what she was told to do against her better judgment. She felt she had no choice and could only think of the financial freedom this closed deal would bring. She felt entitled to her commission and knew without it, she'd be in more trouble than being in a bathroom while her boyfriend potential screwed his own wife. She felt sick to her stomach. She could hear Blondie telling her to put her big girl panties on and suck it up on so many random occasions.

"Hey ba."

"What the fuck! Where are you?" He spoke to her as if she was the lowest form of life.

"I'm in the room." Nervously, she tried to sound convincing.

"I just knocked on the door!" Kevin was more than annoyed.

"I guess I was in the bathroom, I didn't hear a thing. Come on up. Did you talk to Julia?"

Janae was making small talk to get Kevin to bring his phone with him. She needed to keep him on the phone to ensure he would have it in the room with him.

"Why? Did you? You better not be bothering her anymore, messing our shit up!"

"No no no! I didn't call your precious Julia. Just come up here and let's have some fun."

She opened the door and snatched him into the room by his shirt. He snatched back from her.

"Did you call her back and apologize?"
"Yes, now give me some of that good birthday boy!"

She poured wine into glasses. They kissed then she finished her wine. He did the same. Janae laid Kevin on the bed and straddled him. He didn't usually drink with anyone but secretly he was a social drinker. He was so scandalous he never let anyone make him a drink except Janae, he trusted her fully. They had another glass but Janae pretended to drink hers but poured it out on the floor beside the bed when he wasn't looking.

"Come here baby! You ready to scream?"

The bathroom door opened. Julia walked in scared as hell. She did very well walking in seductively, heels still on and very poised for the job ahead.

"What the hell is this?"
"Well, I called her to apologize for lying *(in her as sexy as a*

kitten voice) and I asked her to join us." Janae explained, "Yes since it's your birthday you should have your fantasy fulfilled. I told her a threesome was your fantasy."

"Don't be alarmed. I'm only doing this because you two are legally married and I figured that kinda makes it ok. Actually, I am the third wheel and if you want this, I love you enough to do it."

Julia kept her composure but was as nervous as a cat on a hot tin roof. She was now a liar too. Man she never knew she could act so well. Nine million dollars is a good motivator.

"Is this true Julia? You ok with this?"

He looked very puzzled. Kevin was so predictable in many ways. While he thought he was extra slick and more than good at deceiving everyone he met, Janae had capitalized on his one true weakness. Sex! He was so caught up in having both his women, together in the same room, willing to sex him together no less, that he lost all sense of judgment. He never saw the freight train that was about to hit him. Truly he did have some feelings for Julia. He did want her. Initially he didn't want to pick her for the scam. He was forced to prove to Janae that he didn't have it bad for Julia, so she became the next mark. He really was torn, evil, but torn.

"Yes, I understand. I know you're torn, you two have history. She told me it was your birthday and that she begged you to come here for a birthday surprise."

"I explained to Julia, that you only agreed to meet me here because I promised I would sign the papers right here and now."

Julia walked to the bed and joined them in bed. She was so nervous she trembled. She had to say something or he might be on to them.

"Be patient with me. This is so not my thing."

She started kissing Kevin on the chest and neck. The wife inserted herself between them and started kissing Julia's neck and breast. It took everything in Julia not to scream, gag, and slap the shit out of Janae. This must end soon or Julia would get out of there and quick! As Kevin watched, he got dizzy and passed out. Janae jumped up from the bed. Julia wiped the feel of Janae on her off as best as she could.

"Quick Julia! Get dressed and take that bag of lies from the bottom drawer *(she pointed to the dresser)*. Take it home and put it away. When you come back, take off all your clothes and be completely naked. I'll go to his car, get the transaction papers from his briefcase, and make copies at Kinko's down the road. I will meet you back at your house with your copies. Then we'll both come back here and get into bed naked. He will think we all had great sex and he passed out from the red wine. It's his weakness. I've got some of his semen in my purse. We'll have to put it on both of us and on him too."

"You drugged him? *(Looking at Janae in surprise)* What the hell are you doing with semen? That's disgusting! Hell no!"

"Don't even ask. Come on, let's get going!" Janae's laughter cut through Julia's core. Janae was so smug Julia wanted to knock the smug off of her.

Julia followed with grave reluctance. Janae drove Julia back to her car around the corner. Julia, now high on adrenaline, heart beating super-fast, shook off what she was just told and followed suit. They began the next phase of Janae's plan. Julia got home and panicked. She paced the floor back and forwards. She realized the trouble she was in. Did she want to hold this deal together this bad? Why would she go along with such a ridiculous plan? How'd she get here? He's not even all that! He lacks education; he is obviously broke as hell! He's a con artist! A scammer! A liar who had taken from her and cheated on her! Shit! All good reasons why she should see this through. She had to see this through.

Oh my God she thought! What if Janae double-crossed her? What if she didn't show up? What if this was another part of her scheming plan with Kevin's sick ass? They could be laughing at her right now? She went for her purse and then…

"Hey, *(Julia was caught off guard as Janae stood there in her home) s*orry I scared you, the door was open, and I just came in. Here, didn't want to use my key. *(Laughter)* That asshole gave me a copy of your key. You might want to get your locks changed."
"That's messed up! Anyway, no problem you're in now, I didn't realize I left the door open. Let's look through the stuff."

Julia shook her head at Kevin making and giving copies of her key, she knew she'd change her locks as soon possible. Janae has lost her damn mind walking right into her home. She could have knocked! Julia was secretly fuming.

"No! There's no time. We gotta get back. He could wake up anytime now. Put this stuff away and we will meet up tomorrow when he goes to see the baby momma. You should look it over tonight and see if anything sticks out. I won't understand the technical stuff like you might."

Julia hid the papers and they headed out of her bedroom door.

"Ok, you're right. Let's go. One more thing."

"What?" Julia was afraid of what Janae would say next. "No more surprises please!"

"You've been here before?"

"Yeah he thinks your house is awesome and showed it to me. It is very nice, I wanted one like it."

"Did yall um--"

"No. No, we didn't have sex in your house Julia, we didn't have time anyway, but we did want to. Sorry I was ever here without an invitation from you. I really am."

Julia felt the apology was genuine. She shook her head in acceptance. They left.

"Thanks for helping me. I mean, you're a hell of a lady. I know you're loaded and really could survive without this money. You're everything he said you were. At first, before that other night when you heard us talking, he said good things about you. He never called you a bitch. Honestly, that's when I knew he fell for you. He always said you were classy and I should be more like you. He spoke of you with love in his voice. I was angry because truly I saw him falling for you. I think he knew he couldn't change himself enough to keep you or I honestly feel he would have left me and planned to actually go after a real relationship with you. He's just toxic, sometimes more to himself than anyone else. I'm so sorry we did this to you and--"

"Don't worry, it's ok. Just go! There's no time for this. *(Julia took a deep breath and softened her voice)* But thank you, those words mean a lot right now. I'm right behind you."

"You love him don't you?" Janae's smile was weak and hopeful. She was desperate and curious to know how hard Julia had fallen for her deceitful husband.

"I did, yes, Janae I think I did love the guy he presented himself to be. But, not the one you love so intensely."

Julia turned and walked down the hall. She exhaled and knew things would get better from here. Janae was alright. A little rough but her insides seemed alright. She didn't have to try to make Julia feel better. Julia could sense that underneath her foul mouthed rough exterior, Janae was just a lonely attention starved girl who loves the wrong man. Janae got caught up. Julia imagined that the first con she and Kevin did took a toll on Janae. She wondered how Janae came to accept his affairs with other women for money. That was a life Julia would never think any woman would sign up for. Guess Janae simply got caught up and saw no other options.

As they passed through her living room, the large painting Kevin had given her caught Janae's attention. She cried as she stopped before it. She turned to Julia.

"Julia where'd you get this?"

"From our man" Julia chuckled at her sarcasm.

"Yup, he loves you for real." Janae fell to tears and wiped them as she sniffled out those words. "He bought this at an art show in California years ago. After being immediately attracted to it, he spent a small fortune on it at a time when we didn't have much. When we broke up the first time and every time thereafter, it's the only thing he ever took with him. He always bought new clothes and anything else, but, never would part with this. To give it to you, must mean--"

"Janae *(holding her shoulder)* I don't think he loves anyone. Take it; it's more yours than mines." Julia comforted her boyfriends' wife and felt so much remorse for ever succumbing to his lies. Janae is the one who loved the 'real' Kevin. She knew everything about him and still loved him. Her hate for Kevin was again renewed as she held poor lost and misguided Janae.

Janae sniffled and wiped her tears while Julia grabbed the art and took it with them. Julia felt sorry for her. She wanted to pray but knew God was seriously frowning at her right about now.

On the drive back to the hotel, Julia realized that her own lies kind of started this whole mess. She was near broke herself. She was hanging on by a thread. She'd closed three of her 4 offices and could barely pay to keep the main office open. Had she played a role in this whole scheme? Letting on that she had it together. Spending too freely during hard times? No, she thought! I will not own this! He targeted me and took full advantage of me! I will not take a loss here!

Julia parked back at the restaurant again and Janae scooped her up. They hurried back into the hotel. She went inside. Julia got naked and rustled her hair. Janae went in quietly and sprayed both their hair and bodies with salt water in a spray bottle. Where did this girl get these devilish skills? Julia was amazed, disgusted, but amazed. Janae took a tube from her bra and while removing her clothes she handed the tube to Julia.

"Wipe this on your flower pot."
"Huh?" Julia was puzzled as she mouthed the word.

"It's lubricant. You need to feel wet. He will check."

Julia reluctantly did as she was told. Janae handed her a different tube next.

"What's this?"

Janae tilted her head to one side as if to say 'you know what it is' and Julia knew it must have been the semen Janae spoke of earlier.

"Wipe this on your inner thigh and near your junk." Janae did the same, Julia refused to touch it or use it anywhere on her body.

"Ugh! Geez!" She looked angry all the way. Julia simply couldn't touch what she thought was semen.

"Give me that! *(She took the vial and poured most of the contents on her hand and forcibly she rubbed it on her own thighs and her own junk. She handed it back to Julia)* Now do it! Don't ruin this. Read the tube, it's brand new and it's a lubricant, just a heavier one from the sex store. I threw in the semen comment just to rustle your uppity ass feathers! Now, calm down!"

"I can't, I can't." She sobbed.

"Look bitch, get your damn money! You ain't dealing with no dummies. HE   WILL   CHECK! He's gonna wake up soon. Shit better look like it went down in here! Trust! Now here! Do it or I will! $9 million dollars right?"

"Give it to me! *(Julia snatched the tube)* Ok! Ok! Give it to me."

Julia snatched the vial and rubbed some of it between her legs and on her breast and thighs. Rigorously, she rubbed it on then gave it back to Janae. She was so torn between good and evil.

"You got enough Julia? Your shit better feel wet or he will be suspicious."

Julia put more on just in case. Janae hid the lube and gel inside of Julia's purse. Kevin would never go into Julia's purse. He respected her and trusted her.

"Now hurry get on one side and me on the other. We will both have to cuddle him."

Janae had rubbed the stuff on Kevin's manhood too. Julia's mind was racing with thoughts of how Janae knew how to be so devious. Had Kevin taught her this stuff? They lay there 20 minutes, butt naked. Julia was so tired she really fell asleep. So did Janae.

Julia felt movement and opened her eyes. He was awake. Her heart beat so fast that she knew it wasn't good. She was terrified. Would this work? He rubbed her shoulder and moved his hand over her breast. He stopped at the sticky residue on them. He smiled. Damn he was freaky! He moved his hand down to her vagina. It was welcomingly wet. He was pleased. Julia was relieved and almost exhaled harder than what was normal. She was very relieved. He reached over to Janae and did the same with his other hand. Julia thought to herself "Nasty bastard!"

"Ready for round two?" Kevin said with a yawn.

Julia panicked. She jumped up. She grabbed for her clothes. She'd had enough. She could no longer be there with them, their third wheel in some sick and torrid scheme to out-scheme them.

"This was a big mistake! I don't know what I was thinking. I'm not into this! You need to get a damn divorce, or stay together, or whatever! I don't care! Don't call me, text me, email me, nothing! She will never sign the papers! How did I fall for someone so messed up! Make up your damn mind!"

"Wait Julia, I will sign right now. Watch."

Julia was back in character, this was Janae's cue to sign the papers urging Kevin to sign too. Janae got what she wanted. Janae pulled the papers out of her purse. She signed them. She gave them to Kevin and motioned him to sign too. He did. Not knowing this was Janae's way to secure her freedom from him. For seconds Kevin and Janae didn't say a word. Julia looked at them and pitied them. She then left.

Funny thing is she really meant every word. It was pure reaction to the situation. She knew it was over. She'd never be with him again. Had he just been some married man she fell for, those words, that scene she performed would have meant something. But reality set in. He was a low life con artist and she was his mark! His prey! His target! The walk around the corner to her car was soothing. Julia drove home crying again the entire way home. She wondered, how in the hell did she get here?

Should Have Peeped His Game

Sunday night, Julia found herself needing to hear a familiar voice. She called the sisters, her sisters. She knew it could go either way, but, she needed to hear another opinion about her mess. It wouldn't be cute though. She was ready to talk. They would do more arguing amongst themselves than listening to her anyway. Still, Julia was desperate and needed multiple views about her decision to sleep with the enemy (taking to Janae's plan) from people she loved. She called them anyway.

She could hear all of the laughing and giggling from outside. Her heart was not ready for this.

"Hey hey hey sis, what's up girl? We all here. Whose ass we gotta kick? Got my tenny-shoes on!" Lena, the second oldest, said playfully but seriously.

"Lena chill your ass out! We are here to listen. Come on Julia tell us what happened." Mary was the oldest of them all.

They all exchanged hugs and headed to her kitchen. They sat at the bar waiting for Julia to speak. Lena gathered cold drinks from the refrigerator.

"Yeah cause I don't do fighting." Yolanda was the youngest and the scary one.

"Naw trick, (*Lena was instantly pissed off, she snapped her fingers at Yolanda*) uhn uhn! You shut yo ass up! You shouldn't even be here. Scary ass! See now you done got me started!"

"Damn Lena, what? I got just as much right to be here as you!" Mary asserted in defense of Yolanda towards Lena, who always targeted and bullied everyone.

"Damn! Can't yall table that shit for a second. We are here to listen to Julia. She called us here to help her. Come on girls." Mary's voice was reasonable and direct but nothing calmed Lena.

The sisters all started talking at the same time. Julia immediately placed her hands over her face in despair. She wiped her face and moved towards them.

"Ok! Ok! Ok! Look everybody, just leave. I don't know why I called yall asses anyway!" Julia, instantly fed up, stood up and pointed to the door.

"Girl, come on. Don't trip over them. You called for a reason. Must be important. Like it or not, we are your sisters. We got your back. Now come on, tell us." Mary replied in a concerned voice.

Everyone was instantly quiet. Julia walked back and forth the length of her kitchen. She really needed to weigh some things out and quickly realized that asking for their unbiased transparent advice may have been a big mistake.

"Well, I was at Kevin's mom's house. Had a great time, left feeling good. Then his wife called me."

Julia paused to see if everyone caught or absorbed the wife part. The words burned her throat as they escaped her mouth. She felt sick.

"Wife?" Mary was shocked and confused as were the other sisters.

"Awe hell no! Ima fuck him up! Just wait til--I" Lena wasted no time going from zero to one hundred.

"Shut up Lena, let her finish! Julia are you serious? I like him. Is he really? Did you know?" Yolanda tried to understand and stifle Lena at the same time.

"Julia we're sorry, we're just shocked." Mary comforted.

"It's ok guys, I know. I'm shocked as well. No, I had no idea. I was leaving when--"

"Oooooohweeeeee*! (Lena couldn't keep her cool)* I knew he was garbage! I knew it! Damn! Damn! Damn! Girl lets go kick his ass! I can call Tank-en-nem!"

"Damn it! *(Mary said as she motioned Lena to hush)* Ok Lena, enough! What happened next Julia? You were leaving and--"

Lena paced back and forth pounding one balled up fist into the other hand over and over again,

"I'm gonna kick some ass today! Watch! Watch! We are Whitney's! We kicks some ass when we have to!" Lena's anger rose.

"Well, *(Julia shook her head at Lena)*, the wife, Janae, called me. At first I thought it was a joke. She knew so much about me. *(holding back tears)* I listened to her. She told me how she and Kevin were using me for my money to live off of. Said they'd been hustling women and men for years. Said he promised--" Julia stopped to swallow. Her throat closed and her tongue stiffened hearing her own words out loud was deafening.

Lena was squirming in her seat, dying to kick someone's ass, trying to keep her mouth shut. Mary was holding Julia's hand, also trying to simply listen. Yolanda was dying a thousand deaths and with tears in her eyes that hadn't fallen yet, she spoke.

"Julia how'd they spend your money? How'd they get it?"

"I loaned some and other times I let him use my petty cash atm card. Not a lot of money in it. Maybe less than $5,000."

"What! (*Lena yelled as loud as she could*) FIVE THOUSAND DOLLARS!!!! Yo ass is crazy and stupid! *(She threw her hands up into the air and held both hands to her temples).* You let a dude hold a card with that kind of cash on it? That's fucking crazy! You deserve--"

"That's it! I don't need this from her! I knew better! I should have known wayyyyy better! Get your ass out of my house! Now!" Julia was done and trembled as she yelled.

The sisters all started voicing their opinions and Lena was super hot now. She was boiling. Mary was begging everyone to calm down. Yolanda was crying and got her purse.

"See Lena you always do this! Damn! We are sisters! This shouldn't be like this!" Mary was very distraught.

"Well Lena's right!" Yolanda agreed with Lena.

"What? What did Yolanda say? You silly ass girl! Lena don't give a shit about you half the time! Are you serious?" Julia was pissed.

"Well, it's just not smart to get financially involved with men you are just dating." Yolanda spoke quietly and sheepishly as spoke her mind.

"Really? Really?" Julia repeated over and over again.

Anger rose as she pushed both hands towards Yolanda who jumped away from her path.

"Get out! Get out now and you try to figure out why your broke ass boyfriend don't work and lives off your paycheck! Get your ass out of my house!"

Lena was laughing profusely, so hard she was crying real tears.

"Come on sis *(Lena said to Yolanda)* let's go get a bite to eat or something. Good luck Jules, you'll need it!" Still laughing, she took Yolanda's arm into hers.

"Yolanda, call me when she turns on you next and kicks that ass again like she did last month!" Julia yelled after Lena and Yolanda as they left.

Yolanda looked back at Julia worried. Lena still laughed on the way to the car. Julia could still hear her. Mary and Julia sat down. They were quiet for what seemed like hours but was just a few minutes.

"Look Mary, I can't do this right now."

"It's ok (*Mary stood to leave*) I'll call you in the morning, check on you then. I'm wiped out too. You know Lena would die for you right?"

"Yeah I know."

"You gonna be alright Jules? You got rid of him right?"

"Yep, I'll be fine. And yes, I broke it off."

Julia didn't have the courage to tell Mary everything. She would be so disappointed in Julia for lining up with Janae. She'd freak out and probably call their parents or something. She would certainly try to convince Julia to stop. No one knew she was in trouble financially. She was losing everything if this deal didn't go right. Her pride wouldn't let that happen. Lena would have a field day with this information and Yolanda would just worry.

They hugged and Mary promised to call her later to check on her as well as in the morning. The shower she had before the sisters had arrived still left Julia feeling dirty. She drew a very hot bath and got in. It was sudsy and full of bubbles. The heat resonated through her entire body. It was a welcomed feeling after the day she had had. Hoping, wishing, and praying to rid herself of the dirty day she had today. Her iPod played in the background; her favorite hand selected tunes were flowing from the speakers. Julia was very weak, so broken from Kevin's lies that she could actually feel physical pain. The longer she sat in the hot bath the weaker she became. Her movements were slow and unintentional. She was full of the kind of pain one feels when you give your heart to someone who takes it and breaks it.

Janae's words cut like a knife. His lies were so deep. She had grown to love him; she was in love with him. She knew for sure now that she had fallen hard. Even though she had never muttered the actual words I love you to him. His name on her caller i.d. excited her; his voice on the phone warmed her to the core. He was very smart, why did he do the things he had done? She'd have given him all of her. She trusted him. He made her trust him. As the music played, Julia looked over to a photo of Kevin he had placed there. He stared back at her as if he was a decent person.

How'd you do this? How'd you lie? (Her words went out to him). Oh Kevin! How'd you do any of this! I thought our love was strong? Liar! Liar! Liar! I loved you! I trusted you!

She sobbed loudly, uncontrollably. The iPod played Aretha Franklins "Don't Play That Song". The words brought coarse tears to her eyes. Aretha's soulful sound caused Julia to break down even more, the words bellowed out,

Don't play that song for me, cause it brings back memories. Of the days that I once knew. The days I spent with you.

She could remember so much about their life together these past weeks. *Oh, no! Don't play it. Fills my heart with pain.* She wished the pain would stop.

As Aretha sang that song, Julia's time with Kevin passed before her. She relived their entire courtship. The walks in the park, all lies. The fun times playing putt putt golf, lies. Him washing her car, lies. Working out together, lies. Them praying together, all lies. The first time they met, lies. He lied to her a thousand times.

Cause I remember just what he said. He said Darling I love you. Julia knew that he lied.

I remember on our first date. Julia remembered their first date. Now she remembers it as a lie.

A hot bubble bath usually comforted her. As the water cooled down, it usually became relaxing.

She would describe what she felt right at that moment as a piercing pain. She wanted it to stop. The words hurt so deeply they caused the tears to burn down her cheeks. Felt like death, a sick twisted hurt that no one should feel. He lied. He was probably the biggest liar she'd ever known. He made love to her, he touched her! She met his family, his mom. His mom? She was also a liar. She knew, she had to. He faked a suicide, spent the day with this pregnant lady. Julia couldn't see the bathroom for the cloud of tears in her eyes. She could see Kevin's picture. She picked it up taking all her strength she threw it across the bathroom. It landed on her shower door and the glass door gave way and crashed to the floor. She didn't even react.

She rose completely from the bath tub, slowly because her body was heavy with pain, so heavy she could barely lift her legs over the tub. Her head hung low, her back hunched over in shame, her arms heavy and low as well. She sang to the words of Aretha's song in muffled pain. "Oh darling you know that you lied". Julia stumbled and fell hard on her floor. She came to her knees and as the iPod changed songs to Aretha's Amazing Grace, she lifted herself and knelt down beside her lavish Jacuzzi tub. She prayed, she cried. It hurt. She loved him. She remembered watching Kevin as he kissed his wife. She saw and felt their love. She shouldn't have been there. She shouldn't have seen that. She ignored the broken glass as if it wasn't there and wrapped herself in her satin bathrobe; she carelessly walked to the mirror and stared at the stranger before her.

It was nearly 11pm when she realized the time. She was happy she at least had the great idea to call that Wayne the locksmith guy to rekey her entire house and office again. She remembered Janae had told her Kevin made copies of her home key and distributed them or at least gave one to Janae. What the hell? Some nerve. Julia's stomach ached at the thought. Wayne the locksmith changed the locks on her home doors and both back doors and her garage.

Later she relaxed and read her bible. Suddenly, she heard keys at her back door. She looked out the window and saw Kevin. He was trying to let himself in with "his" key just as she knew he would.

She headed towards the back door to answer it. On the way, she prayed and asked God for forgiveness and help. She geared up for round two. She wasn't an actress but sure had better act like one today. One thing for sure, Kevin Jones was part of the deal that would earn her a check for $9 million dollars and she wasn't going to let silly emotions get in the way of that! She also had several other deals he had referred to her. She needed to keep her cool. Money is a great motivator.

Julia softly whispered to herself, *"He's so predictable!"*

He Lied to Me 1000 Times

The banging on the door was getting more and more intense as Julia made it closer to back door. Kevin was frantic. What did he want!

"Julia you in there? My key don't work! Girl you in there? Julia! Julia! Julia!" Kevin banged on her bedroom window.

"I'm coming! Stop yelling! *(She opened the door)* What do you want Kevin!"

"Well, you left all wrong. I didn't know if I should come after you. I gave you your space. I have been calling all night."

She had no idea where her phone was now. Had he tried calling her? The only thing on her mind was how Janae said a few hours ago that they went to a movie with their kids. Visions of the birth certificates raced through her head. She was numb towards him.

"Yeah, where you been?"

"I went to the park, walked a bit, and cried a lot. I took Janae home after we dropped off her dad's truck, before the walk though. Told her everything was over that I love you. She cried. I thanked her for signing the papers. She said she would walk away totally for $50k. So when we close Thursday, I'll pay her and she's gone. You mean everything to me."

Lies! Janae had a different version of this story. After Julia left the hotel, she and Kevin had great sex, after all she was still his wife right? They dressed and he followed her to her parent's house. There they gathered their kids and they went to a movie. Afterwards he said he was going to see me and make sure "we" were ok. He took the divorce papers and tried to keep them, she insisted on keeping them until the deal closed and she would file it. He was cool with that. Janae knew he wanted to be with the baby momma. He left her and the kids and headed straight to the baby momma. Janae had downloaded the gps onto his cell while he was passed out at the hotel. Janae gave Julia the heads up when he left the baby mommas and told her he would probably be coming her way. How did he keep the energy to do all of this nonsense? This explains why he eats so healthy and always works out no matter what. Obsessively he worked out daily even on weekends. It also explains the lack of sex sometimes. He opts to please her orally then cuddle as if he's some kind of gentleman. Sad. Horrible that Julia had to be tested just in case, even though she and Kevin always used condoms, they don't cover everything.

"Really?" She looked innocently at him.

"Yes baby, that's what I've been trying to tell you. I love you. Only you." Kevin almost seemed genuine.

Damn he's a tired ass liar! Julia looked right through him. He was pathetic! What a bull shitter! The lies continue to flow easily.

"Sorry I changed the locks, I was mad." She lied and almost choked on her lie. She laughed inside. It felt nice.

She hugged him tightly. She hated to touch him. She cringed at the mere thought. He was disgusting.

"Its ok, we can get copies tomorrow. I have to go now though. You're ok right? We're good?"

Bullshit! Copies? What the hell was he talking about! Copies? No way! You cannot have my key again buster! Julia painlessly held back her anger from erupting.

"Yes baby, I'm fine. Where are you headed? Want me to come with you?" She knew he would say no to that offer.

"I wish you could, but I know you gotta work tomorrow. I have appointments all day tomorrow and my mom's got a couple of doctors' appointments too. I'm taking her and will spend the night there."

Julia remembered Janae told her that their kids have field day tomorrow at summer camp, one after the other. She couldn't see any other way to keep him busy while they completed the plan. They needed him busy all day so they could do the final work on their plan. More lies, that she had to accept as he spoke. What a liar he was. Lie after lie, he definitely had lied to her a thousand times.

"Oh baby that's sweet of you. Well, I do have appointments and then I will go to the spa with my sisters for spa day. I need it bad."

"That's good Jules, you deserve it. I forgot my wallet at home, Damn I know, I did it again! I'll give you the money for spa day later tomorrow. Ok boo?"

He kissed her and she turned her lips to allow him to kiss her cheek. He looked concerned.

"Don't trip, I just woke up, breath not good." Julia froze.

"What? *(Smiling)* Girl give me those lips!" Kevin always said that phrase. Julia loved it at one point. She loathed it now.

He kissed her on the lips slipping his tongue between her lips maybe to see if she was lying, she was. She had to hold back from hurling.

"Well, you've got nice breath for someone who just woke up, must be nice to always taste sweet. By the way, today was great, I know you don't do that, but, it was a nice surprise even with all things considered. I'm glad we did. Nice birthday! Guess I came all over the place huh?"

"Yeah, *(Bastard! How dare he bring that shit up!)* you sure did, you're welcome. Happy Birthday. Bye sweetie."
"Save me some of that good pussy. He he he." Kevin laughed a devilish laugh.

He chuckled to himself on his way out. Julia locked the door and rested her back against it. She took a deep breath *(you can do this Julia)*. She ran to her bathroom, and washed her hands face and lips until her lips almost bled. She wanted him off of her. She felt violated.

Strolling through her closet, she pulled out one of her favorite dresses, she wanted to look extra pretty. She had learned a long time ago that men love women in dresses. She'd need all the ammo possible to get Mr. Fontana to even listen to her. Either he knew this thing was a scam or he needed to know. Her plan to show up at his office would prove to be either a very good idea or one so bad it might cost her $9 million dollars. Those were dice she had to roll. She was in agreement with Janae that Kevin must pay. Not only did he lie to her a thousand times but he had started another whole family with a third chick! That must have hurt

Janae a lot. Julia was immune to that part though. She was shocked to see video (*though the quality was awful*). To hear audio of him with the third one, telling her the same lies he was telling both Julia and Janae, made him laughable.

Kevin thought very highly of himself though he wasn't all that he thought he was. He did have flaws. He was unorganized with his wallet, so he wanted her to think. He made bad financial decisions, so it seemed. He drove that awful car, that wasn't his. But, his body oh God was amazing and well kept. So much that it made her want to climb him forever. His smile was warm and his touch was gentle. He was fun, a lot of fun. She guessed that truthfully, they actually bonded in some way. It seemed so real. He was so attentive and accountable at first. It felt real. He treasured her. He acted like he loved her and his eyes confirmed that. It wasn't a little real? The pain grew.

Then there was this piece of expensive art he gave her. It was breathtaking. Julia loved it. It was a part of their connection, but now, she was forced to realize that for him it was all an act. Not even a little real? Did they connect at all? Who is Kevin Jones? She didn't know the least bit who he was. That's what pierced her heart the most, how could he be so cold?

Opened Up a Wound

Julia arrived at Richard's office in first class. She treated herself to a limo ride by ordering a car from a company that had dropped off a small business card sized flyer a few weeks ago. The car was immaculate. The driver was professional, young, well-groomed and smelled nice. She felt like a million bucks. She planned on going to the Intercontinental Hotel Spa after this surprise meeting. She figured she may as well enjoy this lifestyle while she could since it could all come tumbling down soon.

When he opened the door she stepped out hand in his hand, one leg first. Her just-above-the-knee pink dress flowed freely over her curves. She wasn't that big or voluptuous but she was proportioned and valued her small waist and endowed breast. Her hair was flirty yet professional. She wore her Movado watch and Chanel bracelet and necklace, very classy and dainty. She smelled of her favorite cologne, PE360. She loved it and it was her signature. The whole world had gone on from that fragrance, but, it was her signature. Nothing else would do.

Julia arrived at Mr. Fontana's office, with no appointment. He was not the kind of man you see without an appointment. She marched right over to the voluptuous receptionist. She didn't look as pretty as she did the first time Julia was there. This time she looked tired and almost upset to see Julia. Julia handed Ms. Voluptuous a sealed note and asked her to give it to Mr. Fontana.

The receptionist stood up and quickly headed towards his office with few words to Julia. She was gone for a while and came back looking like a deer in headlights. Why was she behaving so oddly?

She was awkward and fumbled some papers on her desk while asking Julia to have a seat. She offered her some coffee in a distressed voice. Julia refused the coffee. Voluptuous tried to hide the fact that she was staring but couldn't. It was obvious to Julia that something was going on. She rose sneakily and looked Julia over from head to toe. Julia observed her actions but remained calm and unmoved. She knew she was flawless and further reminded herself that women often checked her out. She loved shoes and this poor girl obviously didn't know much about them at all or else she definitely would not have made the shoe decision she made today. Julia thought her shoes were awful and if she had nowhere to go she'd take Voluptuous to the nearest Macy's and buy her an acceptable pair.

Oddly, Voluptuous was staring more so with curiosity than admiration. She was registering something Julia had no idea about.

Richard Fontana emerged with briefcase in hand. He walked over to Julia and she rose smoothly. He told Voluptuous he would be back in a few hours. He extended his hand to Julia and said

"Ms. Julia, I'm so sorry I do have to run. I have several outside appointments; you'll have to schedule an actual appointment with my secretary. I'm sorry but it's good to see you."

"But…" Julia tried to interject.

Julia noticed the note neatly folded between their handshaking hands. Mr. Fontana had written her a note? She stopped short of speaking then completed her sentence while carefully concealing the note from view as Voluptuous watched.

"Ok, I apologize for popping by Mr. Fontana."

"Call me Richard please." He smiled.

"Yes, of course Richard, thank you, I will do just that."

Julia scheduled an appointment with Voluptuous the receptionist, for the following day. Once on the elevator, she unfolded the note and read it.

"Julia, thank you for the note. Nothing is as it seems. We must talk but not in my office. Meet me at the small coffee shop on West Gray across from the Brothers check cashing. Tell no one and make sure you're not followed. Thank you."

Julia's heart was racing. She gasped as she held on to the rail in the elevator. She felt light headed. The elevator stopped and Janae walked in.

"I'm sorry, did I miss anything?"

"Where did you come from?" Julia was startled.

"You ok? Kevin wanted; well you know what he wanted. I wanted to try to catch you here. See if I could help."

"Oh, (*she rolled her eyes*) I, I, I, I'm going to get some air. Meet you later I'm headed to meet my sisters for a spa day. Richard left, I made an appointment for tomorrow morning."

"What! Some air? What's going on? What happened? What did he say?"

"He made me make an appointment. Said he was busy all day. His secretary was all weird and creepy. Staring at me."

"I told you don't talk to her!" She yelled at Julia.

"What? (*Puzzled by Janae's anger*) I didn't, but, why the anger? What's going on Janae!"

"That's the pregnant bitch he's cheating on us with!"

"What! You knew that all along? (*She grabbed Janae by the arm digging her nails into her skin*) You lied to me! You fucking lied, again! Damn! Why didn't you just tell me that?" Julia aggressively shook Janae by the arm.

"Don't ever fucking touch me Julia! (*Shaking her arm free*) I swear! (*In a low whisper*) Lower your damn voice! Ok, so I didn't tell you. (*Coy and uncaring*) Do you think you could have handled this, pulled this off in there if you knew?" Janae was in Julia's face.

"How much does she know?"

"She knows a lot, but probably not everything." Janae smarted.

Julia gave her the evil don't-bullshit-me look. She had had enough of the lies. So many lies.

"Ok, Julia I'm just not sure! So there!"

"You don't think she would tell Kevin I was here do you?"

"Damn Julia! You're pretty slow for a smart one. Of course she will. She is his inside connection. Sorry Julia. Really I am. I just knew you'd do better with her, with this, if you didn't know."

"Janae, I'll call you later! Don't forget, delete my calls and messages. Please!"

"Yeah yeah yeah Julia. Ok, I will!"

Julia had the driver to drive her to her car. They drove all the way from Milam downtown up I45 north then towards the Northline area. She made it to her office where she had left her car. She drove off briskly into the traffic. She circled around highway 59 and went to find the coffee shop. She pulled into the parking lot of the coffee shop and re-read Richards note. What does he mean, nothing is as it seems. Nothing is as it seems? She exhaled loudly in a sharp scream.

Banging glass sounded through her car. It was a security guy seeing if she was ok. She nodded yes and he coerced her to move her car. She did.

"You can't park here ma'am!"
"Ok asshole, I heard you! Ok, I'm moving."

She put the car in drive and drove to an actual parking spot. Once she parked properly, she went inside. Richard sat at a small discreet table in the back. Richard stood up and extended his hand.

"Hello again Julia (*smiling a genuine smile*). Thanks for coming (*Julia froze and didn't speak a word as Richard pulled back a chair and motioned her to have a seat*) please sit, something to drink?"
"Yes, water please."

Richard motioned for the young waiter who was nearby hanging on Richards every action. He comes here frequently. She could tell by the special attention he received.

"You sure are a pretty one Ms. Julia."
"Thank you sir" Julia replied with her head tilted down slightly.
"More coffee please (*to the waiter*) and bring Ms. Julia here a cup too please, Julia have you had breakfast?"
"No sir I haven't. I'm not hungry. Water too please!" Julia called out to the departing waiter.

"We'll have two omelets as well, the house special please and wheat toast. (*The waiter exited the table and he turned his attention to a puzzled Julia*) We must eat to power up for what is to come."

"Hmm ok. (*She exhaled, knowing food was the least of her concerns*) Richard, thanks for meeting me as well. But excuse me for being elusive. I'm still in shock, so much is going on and I am not sure where to start, what to do next."

"Julia, tell me, what's going on?"

"Ok. What is your relationship with Kevin?"

"Kevin Jones. (*Chuckling laughter escaped him*) I've known him since he was a boy, full of energy. He was my only son's best friend for as long as I could remember. Of course my son's death shocked us all. Kevin is supposed to be helping me liquidate my assets, and close down my life here. He insisted on being a part of it and I accepted his offer. I plan to go on home soon."

"Home?"

"My family is in Florida."

"Oh."

"This piece of real estate is the last of two very high end properties I have. Both are under developed believe it or not. There is a lot of land beyond those trees. The price is good especially in this market. The other property, Kevin and my son worked on together for years. We've been trying to drill oil on it out in Midland Texas for some time now, years in fact. It is undeveloped. Great buy for someone. Kevin used to be a very bad influence on young Richard. I decided since I could not break the friendship up, I'd take Kevin under my wing and make something of him. You know, help him become something positive. That land out there has been a pain, costing me a lot of money. The reports haven't been favorable and my son along with Kevin, have blotched things up many times over the years. Reports keep coming up with nothing, so they say."

"So you trust him?"

"Like my son, I trust him like my son."

"I'm sorry for your loss, losing your wife must have been tough, your son tough too."

"My son was adopted, still I loved him. My genes don't run through him, never did. I never told him. My first wife and I decided against it. He somehow found out and never told me. My wife told me he knew but, I never addressed it with him. It didn't matter much to me. No one knows but, I guess Kevin does. He's never mentioned it either. He was angry ever since. She begged him to move on from it, he never could."

"Why was he so angry at you?"

"Because I never turned over my company to him never trusted him with much. I always kept control and appointed the best qualified people for the positions of power. He thought I didn't trust him because he wasn't my son, that's not true. His relationship with Kevin was stronger than mines with him. That relationship was destructive; he couldn't grow with Kevin around. His judgment was bad. His temper was worse. He couldn't be trusted with $100 let alone millions."

"I thought you said you trusted Kevin like he was your own son?"

"Julia, if we're going to work together, you must learn to be a better listener. I said I trust him like I trust my son. See the difference? Young Richard Jr. was my brother's son. This sent him over the edge. He badgered his mom until it killed her holding on to his pain. My brother fathered him with my wife, I am sterile and couldn't ever have fathered a child. We wanted him to be family though, so we gave him our bloodline by the use of my brother."

"I see."

Tears rose in the wells of her eyes, what an awful life for both of them, and of course Kevin is at the center of all of this, a catalyst for destruction! He doesn't trust Kevin at all! What is going on? Richard handed her a handkerchief. She dabbed her eyes.

"No tears Ms. Julia, it's the cards we were dealt. In life you get tough breaks but you don't have to break. Kevin is a wild card but sometimes useful. I like to keep him close, keep an eye on him. He likes to slide by and he played a major part in why I never trusted young Richard. He's a con artist!"

"Yet you allowed him to introduce you to me? To work this deal for you? To help you liquidate? Why?"

"You are well qualified, honest, and trustworthy. You proved that by coming here today, to my office, your note."

He handed her back her note with the most teddy bear smile she'd ever seen. He was touched by her, even taken by her.

Mr. Fontana, I am in your guest area unexpected with no appointment, I would be honored if you would allow me a few minutes of your time. There are things going on that you should know about. The deal we are working on has holes in it. I have proof. I hope this note reaches you unopened. Please hear me out before speaking with anyone about this note. Regards, Julia.

She read her note, maybe she even memorized it when she wrote it. She was careful to choose the right words.

"Still why me?"

"Why not you Julia?"

"What do you want? You have to know there are holes in this deal? That they are taking you for a ride, cheating you out of money you're rightfully due. What gives?"

"I want to find my son before it's too late."

"But you only have one son right? He's dead sir."

"That is why we are here isn't it. You have proof he's alive don't you? My son didn't die in that accident."

Julia was stunned. Could Richard Jr. be alive somehow, or was Richard Sr. a mourning father who can't let him go?

"No, I don't know any such thing! What do you mean? How could he be alive?"

She noticed her voice elevated and she quickly lowered her head and her voice.

"I thought you knew? You said you had proof?"

"Ok tell me what's going on? Richard what are your thoughts? How could he be alive?"

"Janae Jones called me a few weeks ago claiming RJ was alive. She said he and Kevin cooked up some scheme to get this land from me. I had already had a hard time accepting his death."

"Janae?"

"Yes, Kevin's wife."

"Yes I know. Go on."

"I didn't believe her because she wanted to sell the information to me and I didn't know if she was extorting money or what. She showed up at my house and security had quite a time with her. (*Richard laughed*) She's a piece of work, nice to look at, but that mouth, oh boy! She had recent pictures of Kevin and Young Richard together, recent photos. I offered her $5000 to go away and never mention it. She demanded $20k and I paid it. I haven't heard from her since."

"I had no i-d-e-a!"

"I don't trust her either. I told her I didn't believe her but would pay her to shut up, so I did. Kevin found out she had come to my house and asked me what she wanted. I told him she was looking for him; she said he'd disappeared again. That was the last we spoke of that. I replaced all my security at the house and have been watching for the breach. Who is feeding him the information? Of course Amanda is a big part of the puzzle."

"Amanda?"

"Yes, my secretary, Kevin's mistress, pregnant mistress."

"Which is why we are meeting here, because she tells him everything?"

"Exactly. Now you tell me why you are here?"

"Why do you keep her, um Amanda? Why not fire her?"

"Because she could prove to be useful as well. Her days are numbered too. Tell me, why are you here Julia? What's the proof you have?"

"Janae couldn't get you to help her bring Kevin down so she came to me I guess. I fell for it and we've been working together to see to it that he pays for what he's done and doesn't get a cent of your money or mines."

"So you fell for his charm huh? You're "involved" with him?"

"Yes. I did (*embarrassed*) we've been, well, a little um romantically involved. Not anymore though!"

"I figured that. Still, I trust you Julia. I knew I could from day one. He is very charming."

"Why? I obviously have bad judgment!"

"It could happen to anyone dear. Because you've got a lot to lose and you have integrity. I could tell when we first met. I knew if there was any trickery in this sale you'd find it. I interviewed many realtors, finally he, the devil himself, Kevin led me to you. See, I told you, he was quite useful sometimes."

They both laughed.

"Thanks Richard, but if I were in your shoes I'd trust no one."

They're plates were empty, She felt a lot better after eating. He was a brilliant man, even stricken with grief he was on his toes.

"You are in my shoes. Let's put it all on the table. Find out why my son would fake his own death."

"Here are the documents we, Janae and I, copied from Kevin's briefcase. Most of it I don't understand. Maybe you will. There's this Oil lease paperwork here, etc.--"

"Oil lease (*he moved the papers closer to him and took a look*) they ended that years ago! What is this!"

Richard read the papers. Turns out the oil lease had continued for 5 years past the time Richard was told it ended. Richard Jr. and Kevin had continued it and urged Richard to give the land to Richard Jr. He said he wanted to develop it or something. Richard didn't trust them to not sell it. He wanted it in the family, not sold. These papers had a company called KRJ Holdings as the pay to party not Fontana Enterprises. Wow! The plot thickens, Julia thought. There is oil on this property! Confusion overcame them both, and then anger emerged.

"Maybe that's why he faked his death, but, how can he… (*she paused and thought for a moment as if she had an epiphany*) oh my God, let me see that. KRJ Holdings! That's the buyer on the sale you're closing in two days! That's it! They've been reaping the proceeds from the oil lease, holding the money to buy the land that you're willing to sell now that he and your wife have died! They can get the oil and also your house! Oh my God!"

That teddy bear look vanished from his face and his skin turned a fiery red. He grabbed his chest.

"Greed! Kevin and RJ would potentially make billions if there is oil!"

"Why me? Why me as the realtor?"

"Because you're easy! (*Impatiently he snapped at her*) Sorry, let me rephrase that, you're independent, an easy target. My guess is he knew you were desperate for business, most are right now. You have no one to answer to. Plus you're honest and wouldn't be looking past the "I" being dotted and the "T" being crossed. Furthermore, you slept with and probably fell in love with the mastermind!"

"Paperwork?" Julia questioned, still not catching on fully.

Julia knew he was right, how'd she mix business with pleasure? She was embarrassed and hung her head low again?

"Yes, about that. Appraisal done independently, survey done independently, both by parties chosen by Kevin! (*Finishing his sentence*) Kevin!"

"Exactly!"

"Now what Richard?"

"Well, you need your commission. I can guarantee it if you'll do as I say from here."

"I don't know, I need to think about all of this. Why would you do that? This is a bum deal! You could just call everything off. You'd be a fool to continue! No offense."

"I am a man of honor, and I know your financial situation, remember I checked. You need your commission."

"So, what's your plan?" Annoyed as she was reminded of his nosy investigation into her affairs.

Love So Doomed

Richards's cell phone rang; he looked at it for a moment and then answered it.

"Hello *(pause)*. Hello *(pause)*. Who's there *(pause)*?"

Julia looked puzzled at Richard as he talked on his cell phone. She wondered who it might be because she sensed some urgent desperacy in Richard's voice.

"Son? Is that you? It's ok son, I forgive you. Please come home son. I know everything. Say something."

Richard was quiet and Julia leaned in to see if she could determine what was going on.

"Dad, I'm so sorry dad. I can't come home dad it's too late for me. How can you ever forgive me?"
"Son I love you, I should have taken more time with you son. It's both our faults. I thought being tough on you would make you strong. Please come home son. I forgive you, can you forgive me?"
"Yes I forgive you Dad but there's more, I need to tell you everything and set things straight. There is so much going on dad. I'm so sorry I did these things to you dad. I feel awful. I love you dad."

RJ was crying into the phone and tears streamed from Richards eyes like water. Julia reached for and handed him back his handkerchief. She too was fighting back tears.

'Son where are you? I will come to get you right now. Where are you son?"

Richard was silent for a long time intently listening as RJ talked. Julia was anxious to hear what he was saying but couldn't make out his words.

"Where are you son?"
"Dad I'm in Magnolia and I…"

The phone went dead. Richard was saddened. He yelled.

"RJ? Hello? Hellooooo? Damn! Hello!"

Richard collapsed onto the table and banged on it with his fist.

"No! No! No! What have I done to drive my only son away into the arms of this life he has chosen? (*Crying*) Oh God please help me and my son!"

He cried out with his hands in the air. Julia moved to his side and comforted him as they both cried. She knew it would be inappropriate to ask questions. Richard sobered and told her he had to leave, he needed to find his son. He told her that RJ said he was in Magnolia but not exactly where.

"Wait. Richard, Kevin took me to see a property in Magnolia. It has living quarters but no one lives there. I thought I saw someone when we drove out there. He said it was probably a deer. I didn't think much of it."
"Oh Thank you! Thank you child."

Richard cupped both her cheeks and kissed them. He looked hopeful.

"Do you remember where it was? The address? Any information? I'll get someone on it."

Julia told him what she knew about the location. She urged him to get the police involved. He insisted she kept quiet about this as he wanted to speak with his attorneys first before he created more problems for RJ. Richard was wise even through all of this, still wise.

Richard motioned for the waiter but Julia told him to just go and she would settle the check. He thanked her, blew her a sweet kiss and trotted out of view.

Julia rested one hand on her forehead for a moment then she decided to pray.

Dear Lord please please please be with the Fontana's right now. Please restore their relationship and bring them peace. Thank you Lord that Richard's only son is alive and well and I ask for special favor over their lives. Please God speed!

That night Julia laid in bed half watching Frasier, her favorite television show. She had tried calling Richard several times to no avail. All of a sudden a news alert interrupted the program.

Billionaire Richard Fontana's once presumed dead son, Richard Fontana Jr., was actually found dead in a vacant building just outside Tomball Texas. It has been reported that

he was hanging dead when found after an alleged suicide.
More details on the 10 o'clock news tonight.

Julia rose from lying down and sat erect on her bed. With her back against her headboard, she placed both hands over her face and deeply breathed in new air. She shook her head from side to side.

No, no he's not dead! No, Richard found him in time.
It's a lie! No, I know it's a lie! NOOOOOOOOOO!

Didn't Last For Long

Richard viewed RJ's body and identified that it was RJ. The body was sent to Florida where Richard's wife and other family were buried. Richard had a gut feeling that RJ didn't kill himself. He also knew who probably had, Kevin. Richard was drained and felt nothing but defeat. Julia called him several times but he wouldn't take or return any of her calls. He was empty.

She went to his office only to find out that he was out until further notice. The secretary, Ms. Voluptuous, grinned as she told her that he had arranged to sell the company and probably would never return. Voluptuous said the words with a self-pleasing tone of voice. Julia noticed her baby bump when she walked Julia to the elevator door. She was purposely checking Julia out again, head to toe. Julia thought, at least her shoe choice was better today. Guess that will save Julia a trip to the mall. She laughed.

Julia decided to go to her office and check in with Ronnie. It was Wednesday already.

"Oh my God Julia, where have you been! I've been calling Damn, I have never ever seen you like this. What's going on with you?"

"I'm fine Ronnie (*hugging her tightly*) I'm fine. Drained, but fine. How are things around here?"

"Awful! Just awful. Twenty more lenders closed their doors since last week. Julia we're in a lot of trouble."

The phone rang in the background.

"Where's everyone?"

"Hold on let me get that, I sent them all home. No need in them milking the clock. *(She hurried to the reception desk to answer the phone)* Hold on Julia. Whitney Realty *(speaking into the phone as she leaned over the desk)* may I help you? Yes, this is Ronnie. Really? I see. Ok, 10 o'clock tomorrow. Fine, I will. Oh, he did? Great, we were not expecting that, with all things considered. Ok, you too. My pleasure, thank you as well."

Ronnie hung up the phone and immediately started dancing, yelling and laughing out loud. She took Julia by both hands and tried to make her dance too. Julia wouldn't join her. She shook her hands free of Ronnie's hold.

"You mind telling me what the hell is going on?"

"We have a closing, we have a closing, nan nanny nann nan! Yayyyy! We have a closing tomorrow at 10! Yayyyy!"

"Who, whose closing?"

"Julia, duh! Mr. Fontana! He called and he scheduled it himself, told them to call you."

The phone rang again. Ronnie answered it and rolled her eyes hard.

"It's your 'boyfriend'." She handed Julia the receiver.

Sarcasm rose in her voice, it was so apparent that Ronnie didn't like Kevin at all.

"Hello." Julia looked fearful at Ronnie.

"Guess you heard by now huh?"

"About Richard's son?" *Or the closing she thought.*

"Yes. That's bad. I'm hurting." Kevin didn't sound hurt. "Be with me. Please. Been days since I've seen you. Barely talked either."

"I know sweetie." Julia held back the urge to gag.

Julia placed her pointer finger into her mouth and pretended to gag herself for Ronnie's pleasure. Ronnie laughed and covered her mouth. She was uncertain at this point, how to react to him or how to handle him. She didn't want to give him a reason to not trust her but she hated him so. She knew Richard must have a plan for Kevin and didn't want to do anything until she knew what that plan was.

"But, tonight won't work. I have a lot of work to do and have to get caught up tonight." *Not tonight or any other night, she thought.*

"Will you at least call me later and promise to dream about me?"

"Absolutely." She made silly faces to Ronnie who was watching closely.

"That's my girl. Love you baby. Can't wait."

"Me too Kevin *(serious tone)* Me too."

Julia hung up the phone and gagged for Ronnie's pleasure again.

"Girl, I cannot wait til tomorrow so I can tell him where to go! I'm sorry I've been so out of character lately Ronnie, I just--"

"Well well well, bout time. *(Ronnie cut her off with a very genuine smile)* Don't worry, I am always here for you regardless of your choice in "friends." *(Ronnie chuckled)* I'm going to get everything ready for you. Will you be coming by here in the morning before the closing?"

"No, let me take what I need home with me please. Ronnie" Julia paused for a moment.

"Yes ma'am?"

"Thanks for everything. I think we will be alright after tomorrow. Be sure to get the preliminary HUD1."

"Of course ma'am."

Ronnie hugged Julia tightly then went to her office, hoping that things were really looking up.

The Closing

Julia was on her way to the closing, working hard to contain all of the emotions rising up inside of her. She was filled with emotions. Emotions of Kevin's betrayal, Janae's lies, Richards pain and grief and hearing the news of his son's death. She fought her impeding emotional breakdown and continued to drive.

Why hasn't Richard taken or returned her calls? Why is he still closing? What is Richards plan? Will he still do what he said he would do? How does RJ's death play a part in his plan? Where will she fit in? He's an honorable man; he must really want to finish this.

She entered through the first set of double glass doors. The building was beautifully made of all glass. She loved this title company. When she made it through the second set of doors she saw Kevin. *How'd he find out about the closing? Surely Richard didn't tell him. Of course Kevin had a way of finding out everything!* He didn't mention a word yesterday.

"Hello Kevin."
"Hey baby! (*He hugged her and kissed her on the cheek*) I was just calling you. Your phone on?"
"Yes, it's on. I don't have a missed call from you. (*She looked at her phone, knowing he was lying, again*) Last call was last night when I called you and you didn't answer." Julia responded sarcastically.

She had missed a call from Janae, but decided to ignore her, for good. They aren't friends after all.

"Sorry baby, I was asleep already. Come on, you're almost late. We already got started. Richard is signing now." Kevin placed his arms around Julia.

"What? It was set for 10! What changed?"

"I don't know, the title company needed to move it up. No one called you?"

"No, not even you!" She smarted him and pushed past him into the doors of the closing.

"Hello, where's the Fontana closing taking place, I'm Julia Whitney, the broker."

"Hey! I did call you; you know how these cell phones are. It's over here. Come on."

He looked slick and deceitful as he led her to the conference room where Richard's closing was taking place. They entered the room and Richard stood and shook Julia's hand. She grabbed him and cried into his arms. She hugged him and didn't care who saw her. She had dreamt of him all night and just needed to let him know how sorry she was for everything he had endured.

"There there Julia. Come on, pull yourself together before you make an old man cry." His Teddy Bear laughed and gently consoled Julia.

"I'm so sorry, excuse me everyone." Julia realized she was doting all over Richard and may have been making him slightly uncomfortable.

She looked around and mostly everyone in the room was watery eyed, except Kevin. He was too cold and smug for tears. The escrow agent showed Richard the next set of papers and said they were just duplicates. She said he could just lift the pages to initial the corners and just sign the last one.

Richard looked over the first page but had to remove the escrow agents hand to see it completely. Kevin, sitting on the edge of his seat, looked pretty intense in anticipation of Richard signing this set of papers. The air was quiet and thick. Julia could hear the clocks second hand tick tock. Suddenly, Richard gasped.

"This is not right. Something is--"

Kevin moved towards Richard and held his shoulder.

"Come on Fontana, just sign. It's almost over. We know you're in pain right now. Let's finish this and get you home."
"Get your damn hands off of me! This was your plan? What the h--" His words choked and stopped short.

Richard grabbed his chest, his heart. He gasped for air. Julia went to him.

"Somebody help him? Richard you ok? Come on Richard, are you ok. Breathe quick breathes please Richard. I think he's having a heart attack! Someone call 911! Oh God please noooooo."

The closing agent grabbed the second set of papers and ran from the room. She yelled, "I'll go call 911". Julia wondered why she didn't use the phone in the conference room on the credenza behind her and why grab papers at a time like this?

"Move Julia let me help him." Kevin tried to interject himself between Julia and Richard.

Julia slapped the hot hell out of Kevin with all of her strength, as he reached for Richard. She yelled at him.

"Keep your damn hands off of him! You've done enough! Just go! He wouldn't want you near him! We know all about you! I hate you! You should be in his place except you would have to have a heart to have a heart attack! You bastard!"

She placed her attention back on Richard. Kevin jumped back, shocked by her words. He moved towards her again but, two gentlemen held him back. These guys were dressed in all black suits, white shirts, and sharp haircuts. No one had noticed their entry into the conference room.

Richards's body went limp in Julia's arms. She tried to administer mouth to mouth but she honestly didn't know what to do in a case like this. The escrow agent had left the room, and Richard laid on the floor unconscious and almost lifeless. She held him and rocked him until paramedics arrived. She rode in the ambulance with what she now knew to be Richard's security team following closely. Where were they when all of this went down? Who are they? Why didn't they stop Kevin? They probably worked for Kevin, Julia thought. As she held Richards hand, he was pronounced dead upon arrival at the hospital. She laid her head on his chest, paralyzed by this series of events, a lost blank emptiness in her eyes.

Lies So Deep

Julia finally made peace with the fact that her home must be sold. Without the Fontana closing, it was inevitable that she needed to do something, fast. She decided to stay with her sister Mary for a while until she found a condo or something while she figured out her next move. Since the closing and Mr. Fontana's passing, she hadn't spoken to anyone except her sister Mary. Mary was a big help, very open minded. Kevin had called nearly every day up until last week. He showed up at her house and she called the police. He hadn't returned but he was still sending her emails as of yesterday. Julia was done. Janae had tried many times to call too. She answered once and kept the call brief. Janae said she had more tricks up her sleeve but Julia told her she was done. She ended that as well.

Julia was moving on. She had already taken a position with a larger firm and sold her book of business to them. She was very pleased that Ronnie was allowed to come with her to the new company as her assistant there too. That made it worth it. She had let everyone else go, laid them all off. She needed to cut her losses and stop the accrual of debt. After she paid all of her bills, she was really low on funds. Kevin had managed to secretly max out her credit cards to the tune of $78,000. She didn't know the charges were that bad until she finally sat down to review her finances, post Kevin. How she let this happen was beyond her. She had trusted him far too much. What she did know was the importance of credit. She had to pay it all off so that she could salvage her credit. One good thing that came of this was the few closings she did have courtesy of Kevin as well as her own rental properties, which she also sold. If not, she'd have no money until the sale of her home which could take a while. So much had happened in this house, good and bad. She hated to leave but vacant homes sold faster than occupied ones. She knew she could use the proceeds from last week's sale of her rental properties to an investor friend, for at least 6 months. Hopefully, once the house closed, she'd be on her feet enough to get by a year while she rebuilt her life. She had put down 30% on her home in a very good market and had good equity. To think, back then, people criticized her for buying the house with so much money out of pocket. Hind sight, she was glad she did. She even cracked a smile as she thought about how that decision back then is her saving grace now.

Knock knock knock, someone was knocking at her door. She could hear loud then louder beating and fist pounding on her door. She thought it must be the movers ready to get her moved to the storage. Why would those dumb asses knock like that! She hurried to the door to let them have it.

Julia approached her glass front door and could only see a figure, the silhouette of a man. When she got closer she mumbled.

Awe shit, what is he doing here, he's gonna have my head!

She hesitated and contemplated not answering and just as she turned to walk away, Thomas yelled and scared the shit out of her.

"Julia open this got damn door! Now!"

Julia opened the door and moved her mouth to say something condescending. Thomas covered her mouth.

""Shut the fuck up! Why the hell are you ignoring me? I don't fuck you! I sure as hell didn't fuck up your life! I've done nothing but be a friend to you!" Thomas was irate.

He had his hands on both her shoulders as tightly as he could, almost hurting her. He released his hands and walked to her living room shaking his head while shoving his hands into his pockets. He was pacing.

Julia thought about how much he really cares for her. Always there, looking out for her, trying to protect her. She all of a sudden got it. She knew he was hurt and she knew she was responsible for his pain. She had been sending him to voicemail for weeks, ignoring him because he didn't like her dating Kevin. She never aimed to hurt his feelings; she always seemed to make a habit of doing it though. Not intentionally, more subconsciously. He was nice, kind, and good and she was a real asshole for being so unfair to him. As annoying as he may be sometimes, he was a very honest and dear friend. Sometimes peoples honesty makes people avoid them. Who wants to hear the truth when they're doing something dumb? Friends do that. She had a shortage of good friends as it was, and couldn't afford to lose even one. She decided right then and there to never mistreat him again.

"Damn it Julia, you just gonna stand there like I'm nothing? Did you hear what I said? I've been calling you for weeks now, texting you, emailing you and calling you some more. I've been worried sick about you! Why do you run from me? I could give a damn about Kevin! I'm trying to be--"

"I get it Thomas (*she cut him off*) I'm sorry. I know. I'm so sorry. (*She hugged him closely*) Thank you, thank you for caring. I've been a bad friend. I will change. I promise. Please forgive me. I really have been unfair. Say you'll forgive me?"

"Alright, alright, alright, enough ok, ok, I forgive you! It's cool. But you have to trust me to be your friend. I know I flirt but I know we are only friends. Now come on, we'll barely make it on time." Thomas grabbed her hand to go.

"On time for what? Where are we going?" Julia wanted to know what was going on now.

"Sorry there's no time, trust me, get your purse and keys. I'll drive. It's a surprise."

"I'm waiting for movers. I--" She pulled away from his hold and pleaded with him.

"NO! Sorry there is no time for that. We have to go it's urgent. Seriously it is."

"Ok! But let me at least get dressed."

"Julia I cannot stress how important this is. Come as you are. You know you fine girl! *(Laughter)* You'll be fine."

Julia looked at herself in her hall mirror. She felt very underdressed next to him all suited up. But, he was adamant about leaving right then so she went, trying to trust him more. Her hair was flat and straight, face tired, no makeup, eyes tired from weeks of crying. Her nails were unpolished, her body clad in a black BCBG warm up suit and sneakers. She felt very under dressed. Thomas was out of the ordinary and unusually forceful. She had the feeling she'd better go without a fight.

When they arrived at One Greenway Plaza, she had a puzzled look on her face. She was confused as to why they would come there. Thomas had taken call after call the whole way there so she never got to question him. She was nervous. But she continued to stay quiet and poised. She felt a little better since she'd put some mascara and lip gloss on, but still not 100%.

He jumped out of his silver Mercedes in a hurry. He'd bought the car after Julia ragged on him for driving a beat up old Hyundai for years. Turned out she'd driven him to upgrading his life, wardrobe, cell phone, house, and if she could have, she would have had him trade in his pretty but stupid wife as well.

He opened her door and grabbed her by the hand and coerced her into the building and onto the elevator. Julia had been on her best behavior, no smart mouth remarks or negative attitude from the house until now. She was all out of patience on the elevator. She yanked her hand from his tight hold and yelled at him.

"What the hell is up?"

"Don't worry, *(he grabbed her again)* we're here because of old man Fontana's death."

"I know, remember I was there! What's that got to do with me? Now? Here?"

"Well, they're reading his will today, now."

"Again, *(condescending)* what's that got to do with me now? Here?"

"My God! You're just a real mess! You're in his will Julia! Now bring your ass on or I swear."

Julia let him lead her but she didn't understand how or why she was in his will. He led her to the Law Offices of Stone and Browning as she read the signage on the entry doors. Once inside Thomas spoke to the receptionist.

"We're here to see Attorney Stone. I'm Thomas Smithers and Julia Whitney is with me."

"Yes, Mr. Smithers sir, they're in conference room number 2, make a right then left. They're expecting you."

Thomas led the way to the conference room. Once inside the attorneys shook hands and introduced themselves. Julia shook Attorney Stone's hand as well and he motioned her to sit down.

Once seated, Mr. Stone explained that they were there for the reading of the last will in testament for Mr. Richard Vermont Fontana. He went on to say they're just expecting one more party and they can begin. Also they conferenced in Mrs. Banks the administrator of The Women's Hope Center, Mr. Fontana and his late wife's favorite local charity.

They then heard the door open and everyone turned to look. Kevin walked in. He shook the attorney's hands and looked to Julia who turned her head. *Julia wondered why the hell he was still in the will!*

Kevin chuckled and as he tried to shake Thomas's hand, Thomas stood and warned him not to go near Julia. Julia smiled inside as she saw Thomas had grown some large balls over these last few weeks. Julia stood with the intention of leaving.

"Do I have to be here? I'm allergic to trash!"
"Yes you do." Both attorneys replied.

She sat down. The officiating attorney went on to disclose all of the assets going to the Hope Center. He read.

To the Women's Hope Center of Houston, my wife dedicated her life to helping women overcome challenges in their lives. She loved helping out there and respected your work in our community. I leave you $1 million dollars in my deceased son and only heir Richard RJ Fontana Jr.'s name and another $1 million dollars in my wife Cecilia Simone Fontana's name. Their recent deaths were more than I could bear. Please open a division to your charity and dedicate it to young boys who need to find their way.

The room was silent. It had been weeks since the newspapers had reported the death of RJ and this was a reminder of that tragedy.

Further Marquetta Banks; I leave you $250,000 for you in hopes that it will help you better the quality of life for you and your family. Thank you for taking the time to personally visit me in the hospital when I learned of my heart disease. I was able to turn to you rather than family and protect my wife from the heart ache of my inevitable death.

"Ms. Banks we will let you go now as per the will. Our office will call you with instructions on what to do from here."

"My God! (via conference call) My God! Thank you. God Bless you all and good day." Mrs. Banks reeled into the phone sounding joyfully over the room like thunder.

Two men in all black suits and white shirts and black ties stepped into the room. Kevin became uncomfortable and squirmed in his seat. Julia had seen these same two men at Richards closing the day he died. She assumed they were his security team. What was this about?

Julia, when I met you I knew you were an angel from heaven. Sharp, witty, easy on the eyes, and mean as fire at times. I was so proud of you and came to view you as the daughter I never had. When you came to my office and exposed the fraud that I was about to suffer, I knew beyond a doubt you were a woman of character and integrity. I grew to love you as a father would his own daughter. You see, I knew I was dying a year ago so it didn't matter to me what happened. I couldn't tell you at our meeting but when my son contacted me he had made a deal with the devil and didn't know how to get out. He lost his life not on our vacation but right here in Houston, his home town, at the very hands of Kevin Jones. I tried to get him out but it was too late. If you're reading this letter, I didn't make it and it's too late for me as well.

Kevin jumped up and the two men held him down by his shoulders. He was very angry Julia could tell.

Julia, I leave you everything I have which totals to around $3.4 Billion dollars in property and liquid assets. I know you'll do what is right with that money and I pray it brings you the peace you seek on earth. I caution you that true peace lies within and comes only from God. Don't ever give up on love. Remember that my darling Julia Whitney.

Kevin, I leave you the lump sum of 1 cent which is all you're worth you filthy lying murderer. Play tape now.

As the security looking guys held Kevin firmly in place, the officiator played a tape of the conversation Richard had with his son on the last day of his life. Someone had bugged the room that Kevin had RJ staying in. They sent the tape to Richard. Richard gave it to his attorney. Richard had set this whole thing up to go down after the closing but, just in case, he changed his will to include this very day in his will. He wanted to give Kevin the false sense of hope that he'd won. It was the entire conversation and the recording showed RJ begging Kevin to let him out of their deal. RJ pleaded with him to just stop all of it.

"You trying to play me?" Kevin's voice was monstrous.

"No, I just called my dad that's all." RJ whined.

"What! You fucked up! You've just cost me everything!"

"No! I didn't tell him anything about you."

"Oh no? What do you mean you didn't tell him anything about me? Liar! Fucking Liar! Even if you didn't mention me, you dumb fuck! He will know I am involved! Do you really believe anyone would think you could pull this off? Damn! Only one thing to do. Sit down, here, take this. Write down exactly what I say."

Presumable Kevin pushed a pen and pad in front of RJ, forcing him to write a suicide letter of some sort.

"Dad, I couldn't go on. I am sorry for what I did. You're better off with me dead. I love you, RJ." Kevin spouted off what he wanted RJ to write.

"I can't write that!" RJ cried in pain knowing he couldn't hurt his dad again.

"Yes you can! And yes you will! He will think you left again. He will be heart broken."

"Oh, so, you're not trying to fake my death again? I won't do that! I won't do anything else to hurt my dad! He said he already forgave me."

"Look! You owe me! If you go back now, he might forgive you, but what about me? He has no reason to forgive me! He will hate me! We need him to really feel like we're both sorry. If we fake you leaving now that he knows you're alive, he will do anything to get you back again. I will be the one to bring you in and we both win. I think that's pretty fair don't you?"

"So we are not gonna fake my death again, right?"

"Trust me man, we are about to end all of this now. Write the letter. I will take it to him. His sadness will get him on our side and willing to do anything to get you back. I will tell him I'm going to bring you home. He will definitely use his power to protect us both from getting into legal trouble. That's all man. Come on."

"Ok, now you're talking! This is good."

Julia and everyone in the room waited for the tape to conclude. They listened on. Then, there was a bit of silence as they could tell RJ was writing and finished the letter. Suddenly, there was the sound of struggle.

"What are you doing man! Stop! Kevin, get that rope off of me! *(Gasping for air)* Man I can't breathe!"

As Julia listened she cried silently at what she was hearing. Thomas drew her nearer to him and kept his eyes on a very nervous Kevin Jones. This was an ah-ha moment.

"You will die today dumb fuck! You just couldn't keep your fucking mouth shut! You had to make me do this! You couldn't let me win one could you! Rich fucker! Tired of raising your ass anyway! It's like having a bad ass kid! Good! Now you die for real! Damn! Die!" It sounded like RJ was struggling and gasping for air as Kevin must have been strangling the life out of him.

Kevin was breathing hard. It's all you could hear on the tape. Then you could hear dragging noises, Kevin was staging the suicide. Unfortunately for him, someone he must have trusted betrayed him as well. Lies.

The FBI agents can now read Kevin his rights and remove him from the room.

"You bitch! You crazy bitch (*wrestling from the FBI agents hold*). You did this! You did this! You set me up! You can't do this to me! I've been waiting all my life for that money! Kissing his ass! Being his slave! How'd you pull it off? Huh Julia? You uppity ass cunt!"

He reached to grab Julia, whose eyes were filled with tears, fear, pain and shock. She jumped to avoid Kevin's touch and Thomas popped up and punched Kevin dead in the face and knocked him out cold. Julia rushed to Thomas.

"Thomas, you ok?" Julia took his hand.

She was frantically shaking. She kissed his hand and they laughed together at Thomas's out of character punch to Kevin's face. They watched as Kevin was taken off to jail for all sorts of charges from murder, fraud, wire fraud, etc.

"Now that's love! You gotta know I have mad love for you now right." Thomas looked lovingly at Julia.

Thomas chuckled. He rubbed his swollen hand as he made agreeable faces at Julia who was mesmerized by his very sweet and giving friendship. Julia's laughter turned to crying into Thomas's arms. She knew it must have been Janae who had sent the tape to Richard. She then wondered how Janae was doing. She was his victim too. She decided to check on her, help her, set her free financially. She begged Thomas to drive her to Janae's house. He agreed to take her, but, warned her she'd have to stay for questions and may have to go to the police station for a statement.

He spoke to one of the agents who explained that they had also picked up the closing agent and a couple of others. It turned out that the closer was a major part of the scheme and left the conference room to destroy the documents which were fraudulent. She had helped Kevin by performing 2 closings posing as one. The second set of closing documents was for the land in Midland Texas that Richard refused to sell or give to RJ. Kevin had gotten the closing agent to slip a new set of documents to Richard. This would be a sale for the land to KRJ Holdings. Kevin would own the house and the land which actually had oil on it. Julia had all of the pieces to the puzzle now. She finally understood the full plot.

Kevin toyed with her to keep her attentions occupied. He "bed" her to get money out of her to fund his life and maybe some portions of the scheme. After all, he did have plenty of people he needed to pay off. Had Janae not called her and had RJ not caved, maybe he would have convinced her to marry him. Maybe he had even more lies planned for Julia. Maybe he would have run off with Voluptuous. She guessed he would have disappeared had it worked out in his favor. He messed up when he crossed his partner in crime, Janae. She and Thomas headed to Janae's house. She wanted to be a blessing to Janae. She needed to thank her for what she did. Janae was the only one close enough to Kevin to bring about his demise. She knew everything about his every scheme. Janae watched him as he watched everyone else.

When they arrived, Julia jumped out of the car, which had barely stopped. She started to run for the door but Thomas told her to slow down as he tried to keep up with her pace. They heard a gunshot. Thomas grabbed her and forced them both to the ground. He held her there. After a few moments Thomas reached for his phone and dialed 911.

"We need help! (*Yelling*) There have been some gun shots fired!" Thomas gave them the address and went on to give details as he held on to Julia.

He held on to Julia, but she escaped him and ran to the house. She busted in not thinking of the danger she could face. Thomas followed her into Janae's house.

His immediate attention went to the sofa where Janae Jones's body laid dead. A single shot to the head by her own hands. Julia dropped to her knees.

"Whyyyyyyyyyy!!! (*She bellowed out*) No God, please no! She changed! I know she changed. Please God!" Julia wept.

Julia caressed Janae's shoulder, blood everywhere. It was an awful sight. She had never seen anything like it before. Thomas checked her pulse. There was nothing anyone could do. She was gone, dead and gone. Thomas held Julia and picked up a note from the coffee table. He handed it to Julia. It read,

Julia, I hope you get this letter. Sooner or later your lies catch up with you. Right is always right and wrong is always wrong. I am so sorry Julia. Tell my mom and dad to please take care of my kids, keep them away from Kevin. I'm glad you got away, the only way I will ever be free of him is in death.

Julia whimpered in Thomas's arms.

"At least she can finally have peace and be free of Kevin and their lies." Julia whimpered out these words in a slow cry.

Thomas held her as she continued to cry. The police arrived storming in, guns pulled from their holsters. They saw the body and grabbed the gun from the side of Janae's body. Thomas handed them the note. They pointed to Julia and asked Thomas if she was the Julia from the note. He said yes. They removed Julia and Thomas from the scene.

Thomas sat a broken Julia in his car and spoke to the officers. Julia cried into her hands, consumed by death.

Home Again

Julia unpacked the last box in her kitchen. She smiled as she stood the last piece of Princess House crystal in her cabinet. She closed the glass door and stood back admiring her kitchen. It was custom built with everything she dreamed of. She moved from the kitchen with perky pep in her step. As she turned on the shower water she gave thanks to her Lord and Savior for saving her, once more. She vowed to live more like the lady He called her to be.

She was a little exhausted from all day visits from her family concerned about the news reports, which she was involved in, that detailed the whole Kevin Jones and billionaire Richard Fontana scam. Her family was now at ease and her parents tucked away nicely at her sister Mary's house.

It took Julia about an hour and a half to make it to the bank. She completed the "Fontana will money" wire process and all of the other financial particulars. She didn't think she would ever get use to so much money. To her surprise for the first time in years she wasn't worried, anxious, or afraid.

Julia pushed open the bank doors and simultaneously checked her cell phone when she heard it beep. She turned to go back into the bank and when she looked up she bumped right into a man who was exiting as well. She startled him and she dropped all of her papers from her hands. She quickly stooped to collect them from the ground. She apologized without ever looking up at him. He was helping her collect the folders and papers too. They both reached for the last paper at the same time and their eyes met. He had the most beautiful smile she'd ever seen. He looked at her as if looking at an angel. He released the last piece of paperwork into her hand.

"Sorry Ms."

"No, totally my fault, my apologies."

"Hi I'm Carlito, Carlito Ray" He extended his hand to shake hers and she accepted it.

"Hello, I'm Julia Whitney, nice to meet you."

They blocked the entryway, taken by each other. Staring at one another.

"Please (*as he reached into his coat pocket*) if you ever have time, I'd love to send a car for you and meet you for a cup of coffee, hope to see you again *(pause)* soon."

"Thank you." Julia was quiet for moments, she took the card.

He was a really good looking man. Whew! He was clean! She could still smell him. He was dressed in an amazing custom suit that hugged his body like paint on a wall. Wow! She exhaled. She watched him walk away then began to read the card.

"Limos huh?" She said to herself.

Citi Streets Limousine
Corporate Transportation Service.
Carlito Ray
CEO

Surprisingly, this was the same service that had dropped the little flyer card off to her office. The one she had treated herself to when she went to Richard's office unannounced before the spa day she never made it to. What a coincidence.

After reading the card, she looked up but she didn't see him anymore. She looked around and saw a chauffeur closing the door to an immaculate Lincoln town car and she could see half of his leg just before the door closed. He was the owner and the passenger.

Julia whispered to herself, *"Hmmm, I kinda like coffee, but nahhhh. No more of that!* (pause) *For now."*

She tore the card up and walked to her car, smiling not knowing she would definitely meet him again.

THE END

If you enjoyed
LIES "Everybody's Got Secrets",
You will also enjoy these titles coming soon by this author

The next titles in the LIES trilogy,
"LIES, Everybody's Got Secrets"
"Before the LIES"
"After the LIES"

The spin off series
"Kevin and Janae, Road Paved in Lies"
"Kevin and Janae, Ride with Me"
"Kevin and Janae, Taking Houston"

Children's Book
"It's Ok to Tell"

Other titles coming soon,
"How to Date a Guy Like That"
"Lash Therapy"
"Sharron"
"The Ratchet Family"
"Shannon's Little Girl"
"For My Daughter if Ever I'm Not Around"

Middle Child Publishing
www.MiddleChildPublishing.com
info@middlechildpublishing.com
info@shannshigady.com
Management: 832-435-8777